Digressions of a Native Son

BY

EMMETT WATSON

THE PACIFIC INSTITUTE, INC. • SEATTLE

Published by
The Pacific Institute, Inc.
100 West Harrison Plaza
North Tower Suite 500
Seattle, Washington 98119
Second Edition
Library of Congress Card Number 82-083162

ISBN 0-9609450-0-8 (cloth)
ISBN 0-9609450-1-6 (paper)

Digressions
of a Native Son

For Lou and Diane Tice,
who taught me that a comfort zone
should never remain too comfortable.

Acknowledgments

Listing acknowledgments carries with it the same danger as attending a class reunion. It is too easy to forget names. Anyone who writes for a living is indebted, in some way, to any person whose path he crossed. How can I leave out, for example, my first newspaper boss, Chick Garrett, who taught me that there is no such word as "irregardless"?

But irregardless, I would like to thank a number of people who made this book possible.

These include the various managing editors I worked for on the *Seattle Post-Intelligencer*—Ed Stone, Berne Jacobsen, Lou Guzzo, Jack Doughty and Bill Asbury. Each in his own way was helpful and encouraging, and they all had an uncommon virtue in common. They let me write what I pleased. Out of this freedom were formed certain viewpoints and convictions that have found their way into this book. The foregoing luminaries are not to be blamed for any of its obvious shortcomings.

I would like to thank Virgil Fassio and the *Post-Intelligencer* for allowing me to use some of the material printed herein. And special gratitude goes to the splendid people who work in the *P-I* library, particularly Lytton Smith; all of them cheerfully gave of their time and skill to aid in research and fact-checking for this book.

Further thanks go to such *P–I* stalwarts as Jane Estes, whose trained journalistic eye gave this manuscript its first hard reading; Jean Godden, for her valuable help and suggestions; John Owen, for his insight and information on matters concerning sports which appear in these pages; Gwen Jordan, whose skilled proofreading caught many small disasters in text. Similar thanks also go to Gena Rochat and to Carol Barnard, both of The Pacific Institute; Gena, for her valuable talent in the book and cover design, and Carol, who supplied the glue that made this book possible. It was this glue that kept the seat of my pants firmly stuck to the chair an ingredient without which nothing much ever gets written. Carol's daily exhortations, shameless flattery, ladylike abuse and simple pep talks helped immensely.

I would also like to thank the considerable staff of The Pacific Institute, in whose offices this book was written. Pacific Institute is a company devoted to assisting individuals by teaching them how best to adapt to change and, most importantly, how to develop their potential as creative human beings. The Pacific Institute staff creatively and cheerfully endured the change of having an alternately glassy-eyed, grouchy, disembodied, hall-stalking, coffee-swilling apparition in their midst. I am grateful.

And special thanks, as well, to Dan Levant of Madrona Publishers, whose overall editing and supervision of the manuscript was invaluable.

Contents

1   Who He?   3

2   The Merciless Trade   24

3   Bloodless Bureaucracy   47

4   Blithe Spirits   54

5   The Voice of Summer   73

6   Long Shot Pete   94

7   Reasonably Honest Jack   117

8   "Orange Blossom"   128

9   Dearly Beloved   139

10   Pillars in Pinstripes   175

11   Purple and White   197

12   Where is Home?   214

13   No Sad Songs   233

14   Mr. Thompson's Bird   245

Digressions
of a Native Son

Who He?

It is always advisable to wear a windbreaker and perhaps a stocking cap when reading the first few paragraphs of any story about Seattle. Too often the prose becomes high-flown and gusty, beginning with lyrical descriptions of scenery in and around the city, followed by extravagant claims for its cultural substance, continuing with much rhapsody about water, quaint ferries, trees and shorelines. As a native, I have no objection to such beginnings. Except in extreme cases when the writing comes perilously close to being bad poetry, little harm is done.

One reason such stuff gets written about Seattle is that a lot of us—particularly natives—actually do become impossibly lyrical in trying to describe the city. July is a productive month for this kind of writing about Seattle and the Northwest. In July, you see, the average precipitation is only .71 inches; so we tend to forget that in January the eternal, maddening grayness produces 5.79 inches of moisture—the peak month of a winter full of clouds, rain, wind and malignant sloppiness.

But give Seattle a few spring days of sunshine and nobody ever heard of winter. Many years ago the historian, Stewart Holbrook, wrote the set piece of Northwest narcissism: "Like many a native, I am privately of the opinion that this entire region should be set aside as one great park before it is wholly overrun by foreign immigrants like me."

Seattle is full of people with an almost orgiastic compulsion toward the outdoors, but I am not one of them. I have never caught a salmon in Puget Sound. I have never climbed Queen Anne Hill, let alone Mount Rainier. I have never walked a nature trail in the Arboretum. My first childhood impression of the outdoors was having wet feet. I still claim the elementary school record, established at Lafayette grade school, in West Seattle, for coming down with consecutive colds in one winter.

Without getting flowery about it, I guess Seattle is all they say it is—a lovely place to live. "The scenery is great but the cast is lousy," happens to be a much-quoted line about Seattle. It is alleged to have been uttered by Joe Frisco, the late great comedian, but Mr. Frisco notwithstanding, it seems to me that the people who make Seattle a city have never been given enough credit.

In a lifetime spent in Seattle, I have come to know an astonishing variety of people. In certain circles I am regarded as an "authority" on Seattle—a notion you are sure to dismiss if you continue to forage through these pages. For twenty-six years my job was writing about Seattle. Five and six days a week, nine hundred words a day. That adds up to 216,000 words a year and in January, 1982 I decided that was too damned much.

Nobody is sure who was responsible for this overkill. The editors who first hired me have long since retired, or died, so blame is hard to fix. Probably the person most to blame for my being a newspaper columnist was a man named Arthur Cummings. His work, begun in the 1880s, had the most to do with getting me into the newspaper business.

In my youth and early twenties I had a vaulting, if unrealistic, ambition to become a professional baseball player. I grew up on the streets and playfields of Seattle, never bothering much about our wondrous scenery; the mosaic of my dreams was the inside of a baseball park. My goal was to get out of Seattle—to Detroit, St. Louis or New York, where I would play major league baseball.

But Arthur Cummings prevented this. It was Mr. Cummings who, in the late nineteenth century, developed the idea that, by cracking one's wrist at the precise moment of throwing a ball, you could deliver it with a downward spin. He is the man who invented the curve ball. This innovation, refined by many pitchers since, precluded my ever playing baseball for money.

But for a brief time I actually did draw paychecks from a professional baseball team. I operated from the safety of the bull pen for the old Seattle Rainiers, of the now-defunct Pacific Coast League. A man named Bill Skiff, the team's cerebral leader, inherited me as his second-string catcher. Since I was what the sportswriters call "a local product," Mr. Skiff was once interviewed by sportswriters on my qualifications. He had a kindly way of putting things.

"This Watson," one of the sportswriters asked, "does he throw well enough to play in this league?" "Well, he is adequate," said Mr. Skiff, cautiously, "I would say adequate is a good way to describe it."

"Does he have enough experience?"

Mr. Skiff said he doubted it. "After all, he's just out of the University of Washington, where I hear he took some classes in literature or English, or something. So he's a little short on experience."

"Does he hit well enough?"

"That's hard to say," hedged Mr. Skiff, who knew it wasn't hard to say at all. Mr. Skiff may not have heard of Arthur Cummings, but he knew I couldn't hit a curve ball. He fielded a few other queries, at which point he felt compelled to speak positively.

"I will tell you about this kid Watson," he said, taking a deep breath. "He does one thing as well as any catcher I've ever seen. I have watched a few catchers in my time—Cochrane, Dickey, Hartnett and Harry the Horse Danning. I will tell you this. None of them could squat better than Watson."

This ability to squat soon was transferred from a catcher's normal position to sitting before a typewriter. The editor of the old *Seattle Star*, a well-known figure named Cliff Harrison, formed the opinion that it would be nice to have a former Rainier writing about his former team. His opinion was concurred in by the sports editor, Chick Garrett, the guy who helped me get started in the newspaper business. Both were probably wrong. But at least I was out from under the cursed legacy of Arthur Cummings.

Since this book is not about baseball, but about the Seattle I know and some people in it, you have a right to scan my other credentials. I was born at latitude 48°30' north, longitude 122°18' west, about two miles north northwest of what is now Runway 31R at Boeing Field. Nobody ever heard of Boeing in those days. My cribhood was spent in a house on a bluff overlooking the Duwamish tide flats. The Indian word,

Duwamish, means "running water," which is more than we had in our house at that time. By going up the Space Needle, you can easily see the bluff on which I lived, but don't do it on my account. It's not worth the two dollars they charge for the elevator ride.

At the age of fourteen months, following the death of my mother, I was taken out of one family and adopted (more or less) into another. My father, the "adopted" one, dug basements for a living. He was a fine man, and my "adopted" mother was the queen of my young life. I loved them both very much, and I was lucky to have had such parents, who may have been "adopted" but were my "real" mother and father. My father dug basements all over Seattle. Going along with him, with his wagon and horses, was my first introduction to many of the neighborhoods that make up the city. It took a lot of rain to stop my father from digging basements, so as a result I got on intimate terms with Seattle's superior quality of mud.

To this day I cannot drive through West Seattle without seeing a house for which my father dug the basement. I also can't read a local tourist pamphlet which tells you that Pittsburgh or New Orleans gets more total rain than Seattle without thinking of all that mud.

During those early years I learned to play a fair game of straight pool after the usual apprenticeship of rotation. (In rotation the balls are sunk numerically, one-to-fifteen, a note I toss in for the benefit of those with a deprived childhood.) I learned to play pool at the corner of California and College because my father kept his own private bottle of bootleg whiskey in the back room of the pool hall. He went there quite often, so I got in a lot of practice.

As a result of my father's profession and playing baseball all over town, I got around somewhat. I learned that black kids went to Garfield High (and no place else), that the "rich" kids went to Roosevelt or Lincoln, that Ballard had a lot of Swedes and that Franklin High, in Rainier Valley, drew a lot of Italians and Japanese. At West Seattle, where I finally started high school, the scholars were mostly white middle class; at Franklin, where I went later, I first chewed raw garlic with a kid named Ralph Yorio.

It was entirely possible then to grow up in Seattle without any significant awareness of such things as ethnic or racial prejudice. Though I liked the Japanese at Franklin, it never occurred to me to resent their being called "skivvies." One of my early sports heroes was a football player named Homer Harris. He was a big, rangy end who played under a remarkable coach named Leon Brigham at Garfield High. Being terribly naive, I couldn't figure out why Homer Harris didn't play for the Washington Huskies. It was only later that I learned that "niggers didn't go to Washington." Instead, Homer Harris went to Iowa, where he became the first black athlete ever to be elected captain of a Big Ten team.

It was inevitable that I would seek him out and that we would become friends. One day I asked Homer why he didn't go to Washington. After all, he was so good, so gifted, that he could have broken the barrier right here.

"Ice cream cones," he said, with a faint, bitter smile. "They offered me ice cream cones." Then he went on to explain. Homer Harris was, indeed, so talented that Washington, which didn't take "niggers," simply had to make some kind of a recruiting effort to get him. "I remember the coach came around to my house," he said. "He didn't seem very happy about being there. And when he told me, 'You'll have to live at home if you play for Washington, but we'll give you books, tuition and all the ice cream cones you can eat,' I knew I'd go someplace else."

One small advantage to being raised in a virtually all-white community, I suspect, is that you live in a kind of vacuum. I don't remember West Seattle as being anti-anything, although its racism probably was deep-seated, just as it was everywhere else in those days. It may just have been that because we were somewhat insulated, it was possible for a young mind to be blank of prejudice. At any rate—and I am grateful —my parents never drummed any hate and fear into my dear little ear. So it developed that names on prominent Seattle stores, names like Druxman, Weisfield, Lerner, Klopfenstein and Bergman, rang no significant bells in my consciousness. I used to haunt Hiawatha Playfield to watch a tall, ambling man named Sam Ginsberg play baseball, attaching no religious connotation to his name. Sam hit long, towering home runs and he was funny and friendly and liked to have kids around. Later, when I was having a tough winter in college, Sam helped me get a job at Frederick & Nelson where I "swamped" packages on a truck he drove.

I once dated a girl named Shirley. She lived in one of the "WASP" neighborhoods near Franklin High School, one of the "rich" districts, and the thing I liked about her was the big sofa in her living room and the active social life of her parents. They went out a lot. One evening after a session on this sofa, which didn't add up to anything that would interest a juvenile court, she asked me a strange question. "Are you a Jew?" she said.

Innocence wasn't a pose I had to feign in those days. "What's a Jew?" I asked. She looked at me as though trying to make up her mind. "Are you just playing dumb or don't you really know?" I must have blushed, because she said:

"No, I guess you aren't one of them. But if you were, you wouldn't be here. My father would never allow a Jew in this house."

Things like that can happen anyplace, I suppose, but it happened to me; it was part of the Seattle I knew as a kid. I don't know what ever happened to Shirley's father, the hater of Jews, but I know that Sam Ginsberg won a shirt-selling contest at Frederick & Nelson because he had so many friends.

The Seattle I knew wasn't at all like the place you read about today. We took its beauty for granted and didn't try to hustle tourists with it. This was before they knocked out those wonderful cable cars on Yesler, James and Madison. Mountains, water, beaches, trees and views were something you had, like mud and wet feet, and you didn't brag about one and apologize for the other. My first hint of Seattle's remote insularity came when I heard Jim Phelan, the hard-bitten old Washington football coach, proclaim that "Seattle is the last stop on the line—when the train stops here, it backs up."

Only later did I realize that Jim was just sticking the deep needle into a service club mentality that looked upon Seattle as the center of the universe. I suppose there is no real harm in calling Seattle "the most beautiful city in America," or nicknaming it "the Emerald City," and kicking pebbles when we get picked as "America's most livable city." It's hard to determine how we truly rank in these matters; I suppose we're in the first division and might even make the playoffs.

Another claim I've heard all my life is that Seattle is "the boating capital of the nation." That one is another booster statement, hard to verify, but again it does us no harm. There are frightening numbers of boats around, but being what might be termed a seagoing claustrophobic, I never had much fun on boats. The only boats that ever gave me much pleasure in Seattle were the big battleships and cruisers that used to anchor in Elliott Bay during "Fleet Week." When the navy came, that was a signal for us to rush down to First Ave. and watch the gobs at work during shore leave. About three good fights a night was average.

The way you got to First Ave. from West Seattle was by thumb or street car, those rattly old orange things. They clanked and swayed over an incredible old wooden trestle, high above Spokane St., weaving and shaking until you had to close your eyes to keep from getting a headache. They came down off the trestle and went up First Ave., and you got off at Pike St., which was the real heart of the city. From anyplace on downtown First Ave. you were within easy walking distance of the waterfront (Railroad Ave. then) and the skid road.

The old waterfront was for real. It wasn't a place for tourists (a tourist stood a fair chance of getting rolled), or boutiques and import shops; it was crowded, smelly, tough and altogether splendid. During World War II, I worked as a longshoreman on those docks, usually down in the ship's hold, stacking cement, lumber, booze and toilet paper, the kind of stuff it took to Preserve Our Way of Life in the South Pacific. As one of Harry Bridges' more reluctant permit workers, I didn't see much that was quaint on the old waterfront. I do know that when the wind whipped off Elliott Bay in January, it was wise to cover the private parts of a brass monkey. Before that I used to hustle the *London Evening Standard* and the *London Daily Mirror* aboard the English ships which came in. There were certain fanatics among the crew who chipped in to pay the outrageous sum of fifty cents a copy to get the "football" scores, and it was only later I learned they were talking about soccer.

It is difficult sometimes to remember that whole generations have grown up with the belief that Pioneer Square is a
neighborhood of boutiques, kite shops, imported furniture
stores, fancy bars, fashion stores and flower shops. No,
kiddies, it wasn't always like that. The Pioneer Square (we
never called it that) I once knew was a gamy and sometimes
dangerous place to be. Tough gangs from Ballard and West
Seattle would roam the old skid road "hunting gooks,"
which meant there was some sort of atavistic satisfaction in
beating up Filipinos.

This was long before the Volvo invasion; skid road then was
a haven for loggers, dockworkers, tree toppers and a heavy
flow of transients. The metamorphosis of Pioneer Square,
whose early, lively atmosphere waned throughout the fifties,
began in the mid-sixties. An architect named Ralph Anderson and a remarkable fellow named Dick White, an ex-waiter
at Rosellini's Four-10, began buying up and restoring old
buildings. Dick White developed a Midas touch rather late in
life, and he probably is the only millionaire I ever really
rooted for. It was Anderson and White who touched off the
wave of sandblasting and renovation to revive an important
part of Seattle not yet smothered by glass and aluminum.

Another guy who did a lot to dramatize Pioneer Square is
Bill Speidel, whose books on early Seattle history still sell
briskly. Speidel, who publishes *Seattle Guide*, a local dope
sheet for tourists, still keeps an office in the skid road. He runs
the underground tours in Pioneer Square and owns a tavern
called Doc Maynard's, named after the amiable pioneer,
much given to booze and collecting wives. Ever since I was a
kid I've heard about the celebrated "Seattle Spirit." "The
'Seattle Spirit,' " Speidel once told me, "consists of a handful of people in Seattle who know what's going on. The rest
we just keep around for bulk."

So now in Pioneer Square, the old skid road, you can buy imported Irish sweaters, expensive French Camembert, tailored leather clothes, decorator lamps and carpets—trophies and trinkets for the invading armies of Master Charge. But in the thirties, you could get a bowl of soup for a nickel, in a place run by a suspicious old son of a bitch who made you put the nickel on the counter before you got the soup.

Henry Broderick used to say, tongue in cheek, "We had a better class of bums in the old days." The late Mr. Broderick, who was a semi-pioneer himself, had his office at Second and Cherry, at the edge of the skid road. Outside of Henry's office was a garbage can where the down-and-outers used to forage. On one occasion, when Henry saw a bum rooting around in the garbage can, he left a meeting in his office and went outside. With a crumpled dollar bill in his hand, Henry joined the bum by putting his head down in the garbage can. Then he pulled up the dollar bill. "Look what I found!" he exclaimed. "Here, you were here first, you take the dollar." The bum smoothed the bill out between his fingers. "Thanks," he said. "I guess some rich bastard threw it away."

Of all the characters around the skid road, few topped Henry himself. During his early years, he buddied around with Bill Boeing when the founder of the airplane company had only seven employees in a barn on Lake Union. Yet Henry himself never flew in an airplane—not until he boarded a 707 on his ninetieth birthday. Henry never owned a car. He spent between $2,000 and $2,500 a year on taxicabs and figured he wasn't too far behind the game. At one point in his life, when Henry was seriously ill in Providence Hospital, a call went out for blood donors. No fewer than twenty-seven cab drivers arrived at the hospital to volunteer.

I was never a licensed delinquent, but I ranked fairly high in the truancy department. An afternoon in a burlesque house was always more fun than a class in mechanical drawing at James Madison Junior High. And there were six Chinese lotteries on Main Street alone. In later, less innocent years, I always suspected that a lot of down payments on houses in Laurelhurst and Mount Baker were made with what it took to keep those lotteries open. The cops seemed to be well greased.

Playing the Chinese lottery was kind of ceremonial, the thing you did when you first hit the skid road. You might hit it lucky on the "short draw." Outside each Chinese lottery was a street shill, usually Caucasian, who'd whisper, "Short draw, buddy," or "Chuck-a-luck inside." Lord knows why he whispered.

The inside of a Chinese lottery was usually spare and uninspiring, except for the rattle of dice in the chuck-a-luck cage. This was for high rollers, meaning guys who had jobs. For a dime you could play the "short draw," winners announced every hour, or "long draw," winners announced once a day. To give you an idea of post-Hoover prosperity, guys used to get up a "pool," by chipping in a penny or two cents apiece, sending a messenger over from the waterfront to play the short draw.

My buddies and I always played the short draw. It took less than an hour to find out if you hit it big for six or seven dollars. In the back room at a long counter you got a green slip for a dime with the numbers and Chinese writing on it. There were Chinese ink pots full of gummy, thick ink and you painted out the numbers with a little brush on a bamboo handle. There was one lottery at Second and Washington; right outside was a police call-in box. The owner of the

Chinese lottery called up headquarters and complained: "That call box is ruining my business. Your boys stop to call in and it scares the customers away." The next day the call-in box was moved around the corner.

The skid road was where I had my first drink of whiskey in a speakeasy. It was also where I first fell in love, or thought I did. Her name was Babe. She worked in a house on Maynard St. near where the Seattle Lighting Fixture Company store is today. She couldn't have been more than nineteen. She had natural, genuine blonde hair, which she wore long, and she had a fine, smooth complexion, about the color of vanilla ice cream, and she was no makeup junkie.

If you came early in the evening, around eight, before the fashionable hour, she wasn't too busy and had time to talk. Babe's boss, the madam, was a congenial old crone who took a liking to me. When I told her I planned to go to college if I could scrape up the money, she affirmed her belief in higher education. She gave me what she called a "student rate," a dollar instead of the usual two.

When she wasn't keeping regular office hours, Babe lived up near Volunteer Park. As most Seattle people know, Volunteer Park is a city showcase, partly because of the Seattle Art Museum, and because of its beautiful rolling acreage which gets a big play in picture books and tourist guides. Until his death six years ago, the art museum was presided over by Dr. Richard E. Fuller, a saintly fellow, whose mother, Margaret Elizabeth MacTavish Fuller, donated the museum to the city and stocked it with a lot of jade and oriental art. Dr. Fuller's gifts, good taste and donations made it one of the better museums in the country.

The point here is that the first time I visited Volunteer Park was not to view stuff in the museum. It was to see Babe. It was the only time she let me see her outside of office hours. We went to the museum, which was free, thanks to Dr. Fuller, and then we walked around the reservoir in Volunteer Park. Babe didn't say much but she looked great, even out of her natural habitat, not losing any of her glamour the way Austrian ski instructors do when they dress up in street clothes and take an honest job.

I told Babe that I'd made up my mind to enter the University of Washington if I could borrow the first quarter's tuition. I told her maybe I could even get some financial help by playing baseball for the Huskies. To impress her, I even hinted that I might pick up a few thousand dollars playing professional ball. This was long before I met some of the more skilled users of Arthur Cummings' invention.

Babe wanted to know how many people went to the university. "The enrollment is about ten thousand," I told her. "A lot of them are women. You ought to go there yourself. Even if you work nights, you can take day classes." "How many guys go to the university?" she wanted to know. I guess her mind worked along special lines.

"About six thousand," I said. "Jesus!" Babe exclaimed. "Don't tell them about the student rate."

That was the last time I saw Babe except for a couple of times in her professional capacity. So I was forced into a grim period of celibacy while trying to get into the university with a 1.45 grade point average. A history teacher I knew at West Seattle was a big help. Ed Liston not only was a history teacher, he was a good semi-pro pitcher, and often I would catch him in a game on Sunday and sit in his class on Monday. Ed sent me out to see the dean of men at the university, a fine old gentleman named Herbert Thomas Condon, who handled special admission cases. When Dean Condon got a look at my high school transcript, it was one of the few times I ever saw blood drain from a man's face. But he let me in on probation.

Growing up as I did, hanging around the skid road, First Ave., the waterfront and dreaming mostly about baseball, it wasn't hard at all to get a 1.45 grade point. But I did get into the university, and Tubby Graves, the baseball coach, got me jobs punching out mutuel tickets at Longacres and later he got me a job at Boeing's Plant One down on the Duwamish. I'm glad I worked for Boeing once, because this kind of puts the "Made in Seattle" stamp on me.

My Boeing interlude was in 1939, when Boeing was building thirty-eight B-17C's for the RAF and our own Army Air Force. Along with these, they were building ten Boeing Stratoliners, model 307, the first four-engine commercial transports. They built five of these for Trans World Airlines, three for Pan Am and one for Howard Hughes. Because of school, I worked the swing shift. It would be nice to relate that I was part of a team that produced the goods that won World War II. The truth is, I never saw anything that even looked like an airplane.

When I first arrived at Boeing, they gave me a file. From four o'clock to midnight all I did was file. Pieces of aluminum —hundreds of them, all shapes—were cut from a template by a band saw. The saw left the aluminum with a "burr" which was jagged and sharp. My job was to file off the burr. Eight hours a night. Four hundred and eighty minutes. It was dreadful, mind-numbing work. A few times I deliberately cut a finger on this burr. The idea was that you could get a half-hour break to visit the infirmary. That's how awful it was. But I'm glad I did it for a while, because I met Manny, a fellow filer. Manny lived on a houseboat on Lake Union and he was a Marxist.

He was my introduction to the way thousands of Seattle people lived on houseboats. There were maybe twelve hundred houseboats then, most on Lake Union, but some of them on the Duwamish River. You'd really be stretching a point to call them quaint, although some of them probably were. I remember that the Duwamish houseboats were called "the Broadmoor of Hooverville," the real Hooverville being a shacktown which sprang up on the downtown waterfront after Mr. Hoover laid his egg. Houseboats in Seattle now number only a few hundred, and some of these look like condos in good neighborhoods.

Anyway, Manny's houseboat was down on Lake Union, not far from where Ivar Haglund's Salmon House is today. As I said, Manny was a Marxist, which indicates what can happen to a man when he has to file burrs off metal for a living. But he was a good influence on me. He read voraciously. He loved to argue and liked to question everything I thought I was learning up on the campus. Manny was really the first editor I ever had.

He would read and dissect stuff I had written, quarreling loudly with viewpoints, syntax and punctuation. One day he said, "You have a way with words, but you must have diarrhea of the typewriter. Read Westbrook Pegler," he advised, referring to one of Mr. Hearst's curmudgeon columnists. "Pegler is a reactionary bastard but he knows how to put words together so they don't run off the page. Maybe someday you can make a living writing for a newspaper. You won't get rich, but it beats hell out of filing aluminum."

Manny was right on all counts. Six years later the old *Seattle Star* hired me. There followed a four-year interlude at the *Seattle Times*. This was altogether a pleasant stop, since I worked with, and sometimes for, one of the best city editors in the country, Henry MacLeod. I also worked with a young guy who used to be around in the early mornings about the time I was finishing up after ball games. He was a fellow I got to be friends with, a fellow named Jim King, who is now identified on the *Times'* masthead as executive editor. We still have an occasional lunch and tell fibs to each other.

The last man to hire me was a man named Lee Ettelson, a tall, impeccably dressed, urbane product of San Francisco and New York, who came here and stayed a spell, making it as brief as he could. Lee was one of those designated hitters the late William Randolph Hearst used to send around to stir up his then formidable chain of papers. Because of Ettelson, along with the managing editor, a fine man named Ed Stone, I settled into a pleasant sort of aviary known as the *Post-Intelligencer.*

Lee Ettelson, whom I privately called "the Spanish Duke," because of his regal bearing and high shirt collars, made no secret of his belief that Seattle was only a generation removed from the Indian ladies who used to rub urine in their hair. He knew all about the egos of alleged writers, and once, when he detected a swelling of my own ego, delivered a pronunciamento which is hard to forget: "A columnist is just a clerk who got lucky. I've always contended that if you give anybody two-column play in a newspaper and let him prattle on every day, he'll develop a following. No matter how bad he is."

The shift from sports to writing about a whole city was somewhat gradual; some say it roughly paralleled the increase in smog above Seattle. But for some twenty-six years, from once a week to three times a week, to five, then six, that is what happened. A crazy way to make a living but a lot of fun.

Some nine hundred words a day, pounding the phone, walking the streets, poking around, scribbling notes, and occasionally getting sandbagged by some anecdote that had appeared in the *Reader's Digest* three months before. I got sued for libel twice and lost both times. During those years the Pulitzer people were strangely silent about my work. But once, when I interviewed George Lincoln Rockwell, the American Nazi, he told me I would be high on his hit list when he came to power. I must have done something right.

Early on, I thought of Seattle as small, provincial and much too circumscribed for my undoubted genius. I begged Lee Ettelson to get me transferred to Los Angeles. Lee may have had his own opinions about Seattle, but he sensed I belonged here. He knew that, in a figurative sense, I was born with webbed feet. He knew that I probably would never be happy living anywhere else. But he said he would do what he could about getting me out of here. Then he added: "I can't imagine why anybody lucky enough to be raised in Seattle would want to live in Los Angeles. But I guess," he sighed, "somebody always marries the fat girl."

Nothing came of this early attempt to bolt. Since those days, I've traveled extensively. Each return home has been better than the last. I've returned to Seattle hundreds of times by air, and always have considered it a lucky flight if the plane arrives a little before dusk on a decent day.

This is the perfect way and the perfect hour to come home. Seattle at its best: the plane begins its long descent south of Olympia, coming down over the islands and beaches of Puget Sound, up along Vashon Island for the wide, sweeping approach to the south. At this precisely right time of arrival, you get the full sweep of it—the mountains we boast about, the lakes and trees and curving shorelines and, because it is dusk, the thousands of cool vapor street lights cutting and crossing and weaving over the hills of the city. Turning in-bound to Runway 16L at Sea-Tac Airport, the plane crosses the "outer marker" of the Instrument Landing System precisely over the parking lot of the Boeing plant, at exactly 1,700 feet from the ground. There, on your left, is Lake Washington, the two floating bridges, and to the west, on Elliott Bay, are the ships and the docks and the cranes and the mouth of the Duwamish River, above which I was born.

Not to sentimentalize, but at times like this I'm glad I didn't marry the fat girl.

Fifteen years ago I made a pilgrimage to Basel, Switzerland, to look up an old Seattle citizen I knew about. I found him in a compound of sixteenth and seventeenth century buildings grouped along the St. Albanvorstadt. Inside was a courtyard and off the second floor living room was a large room with a grand piano. In a smaller room beyond was a large painter's easel which held a bright, uncompleted abstract. The window shutters opened on the courtyard and when he composed music and played, birds would actually fly in and perch on his music stand. He had just returned from a show of his paintings in London and another in Paris, where he received the Order of Arts and Letters from the Louvre—which is the equivalent of the French Legion of Honor for artists and writers. He was formidable looking, a handsome figure of a man, gray-white hair and beard; his speech was trenchant, sometimes angry, often eloquent, a speech of soft rhythm laced with American slang, colloquialisms, and an occasional curse. Mark Tobey was seventy-seven when I found him.

Although Mark Tobey was twenty-two when he moved here, he became a confirmed, devoted citizen of Seattle. Much of his work is a priceless record of the Pike Place Market which I first knew. This was long before it fell into disrepair and its enticing location became so attractive to developers. It was before architect Victor Steinbrueck and a body of determined citizens rallied the voters to save the Market from the wrecker's ball. Tobey had agreed to see me because he knew I had fought to save the Market he knew and cared for.

The Rhine flows through Basel, and Tobey insisted we walk along the promenade. He seemed to take pleasure in pointing out the great old houses and a large ancient church which began at the Rhine's edge and towered upward. But it soon became clear that he wanted to talk about Seattle.

"It is a rare thing when an artist becomes involved in the city where he works, and I became involved with Seattle long ago. I have always tried to say the right things about it. I have always tried to do what I could." Of course I knew that Tobey had donated some of his work to raise money to save the Market. He walked briskly, arms clasped behind him, talking as he walked, remembering Seattle and the Market, remembering "the old men who used to lean against the buildings."

Then abruptly he asked, "Do you know why I became involved in Seattle? It was because of the beautiful nights and the clouds and the salt air. But mostly it was because of the people. The people are what make up a city. It isn't always the place, you know. Tell me," he asked, a touch of indignant sadness in his voice, "are they going to ruin it? Is Seattle going to become another sprawl?"

I said yes, the sprawl was already malignant. But I told him that Seattle was still, for all of its towering, obscene buildings, ugly parking lots and freeways and vulgar signs, a pretty good place to live. I told him that the Market still was much in danger. He nodded, then said: "I worked hard in Seattle, I love Seattle. That is where I made my name. But tell me, what of First Avenue? If they destroy that street, they destroy another part of our city. What of the old people, the poor people there? They have a right to live! Where will they go?"

I didn't answer, but I remembered a shop on First Ave. where I once hocked a homemade ukulele for fifty cents, and how I used to crash the First Ave. Theatre by climbing the fire escape on Post Alley and going in an open window through the boiler room. I wanted to tell him that Turko, the news vendor, was still alive and that the Army-Navy surplus stores still thrived, but I could not tell him what would happen to the old people, the poor people.

"I have a lot of fame," he said, "but not much money. There is a great pull to go back to Seattle, but it has lost so much. They try to save it, but not the right way. Always the big, big effect and they end by destroying it. The government takes their money and then gives it back so they can build those silly buildings. Gosh damn them all!"

We walked for a while, then returned to climb many steps in order to cross the foot bridge which spans the Rhine, moving toward the old part of Basel where Tobey lived. He stopped for a long time at the top of the steps to catch his breath. "I will come back some day when my health fails. What I like best about Seattle are the people I know."

He never returned. Tobey died six years ago in Basel at the age of eighty-five. Seattle had changed too much for him— the Seattle of glass, aluminum, asphalt, and tall impersonal buildings; the march of "progress" wasn't for him, the growing vulgarity that does not alloy well with the beauty we boast about. Probably he would not care that what he was saying is what this book is about: "The people are what make up a city, it isn't always the place, you know."

2

The Merciless Trade

Ever since the days when Walter Winchell was running the nation with three-dot journalism, it has been an article of faith that all columnists lead glamorous lives. A big-city columnist screams things into the phone like, "Stop the presses!" while press agents and politicians approach him on hands and knees, begging a crumb of publicity. The mayor, or police chief, calls on him for advice. A traffic cop would never think of giving the columnist a ticket for illegally parking in a 4–6 P.M. time zone. Certainly not a 7–9 A.M. zone, because the columnist rarely gets up before noon. I was not one of these.

In some twenty-six years as a columnist for the *P–I* nobody ever called and asked me to surrender him to the police; nobody above the level of a municipal garage attendant ever sought my counsel. There were days when nobody called at all. A normal day's work was pretty routine. It consisted of hours spent with a phone to the ear listening to things like this: "Hey, I got a great story but you can't print it." "Here's a hot one, but you'll have to clean it up." "I do okay at lunch, but my dinner business is dying, so how about a little squib? A plug never hurt anybody."

As a columnist for the *P-I*, I sort of resembled Black Beauty, the famous horse of children's stories. I was given a warm, dry stall and enough money to buy bran mash and keep my bar bills current. Occasionally, one of the kindly masters, with offices just under the *P-I* globe, patted me on the head and I whinnied gratefully, but for the most part I was given a loose rein. For this I whinny now. In addition to these benefits I was given a groom, or assistant, usually a she, who acted as secretary, counselor, den mother and copy editor.

Over the years, I had a number of these grooms, or stable hands. The first was a young woman named Sharon Lund, fresh out of college. She was bright, upbeat and very pretty. As a result, I seemed to meet every eligible bachelor in town. They'd come around to cast soulful glances or try for dates, but Sharon eventually married a fellow named Dick Friel and things got back to normal. Then one day she announced she was in a state of pregnancy, so another young lady came along in the role of stable hand.

Her name was Carol Barnard and she was from New Jersey and she was just passing through and she agreed to stay for a month. That was seventeen years ago. She worked on the column for a while, quit once, then came back, and she left her mark. "Stop reading Herb Caen," I commanded one day, referring to the great San Francisco columnist. "We need stuff for our own column, so get on the phone." "Look," she replied, coolly, "on what you pay me, I have a right to read a good columnist for a change."

Carol had a memory like a WordStar disc in an IBM computer. She could spell things like Weyerhaeuser and chrysanthemums aloud without looking them up, although she retained a dignified skepticism toward writers and journalism. Once I tried to explain the way of good writers in reporting the news. "This guy," I said, referring to Barry Farrell, one of the best writer-journalists I know, "is a rare combination. He is a great reporter and a gifted writer. In addition, he's a fine raconteur. It's a rare thing when a writer is good at both writing and talking." "How interesting," she said. "Which one are you good at?"

She had the usual eastern establishment background and one day, tired of being a stable hand, or column curator, she went home to New Jersey. The next thing I learned was that she was devoting her life to teaching kids how to paddle canoes at a Maine summer camp. The new designated column curator was Barbara Huston, who then was married to an Episcopal priest. This inhibited my office vocabulary, but not much. When she applied for the job, I asked her what her background was and she said she had spent two and a half years on the Berkeley police force in California. "Tell me," I asked, fearing the worst, "did you subdue suspects?"

"Not really," she said, "but I once arrested a prostitute in a ladies' room. What I really enjoyed, though, was target practice on the FBI shooting range. I scored very high with the submachine gun. The submachine gun gives one a sense of power, of course, but I do think that small hand guns are more ladylike weapons, don't you?"

Barbara was the fastest draw in the west when it came to answering the phone. She stayed for a spell, then went off to write feature stories under her own byline. Carol Barnard's devotion to canoe teaching finally waned and she came back more or less permanently to keep Black Beauty's stable in order. Probably the only objection I had to writing columns year after year was the dailiness of it. John Owen, who writes six sports columns a week in the *P-I*, plus a popular cooking column called "Intermediate Eater," summed up the racket quite adequately.

"I only take about ninety minutes to write a column," he once told me. "But the rest of the day is spent walking around and figuring out what to write. Everything you see, everything you hear, the stuff you read, is all put into your brain with the thought, 'Is this stuff good for a column?' " Owen, being a meticulous fellow, keeps a file of column fodder notes and clippings, and he has a clear head because he runs three miles every day.

Eventually, if you do it long enough, the column becomes almost a physical part of you, like having bunions or a nervous stomach that won't go away. You don't make friends, the way you should; you make acquaintances and sources. You cultivate people, not on their merits, but mostly with an eye to how they can stimulate column ideas for you. This is not nice. You tend to become reclusive and selfish because the column is an extension of your personality; you become self-centered, since your waking hours are devoted to getting the required ration of words on paper.

People with abundant egos tend to refer to themselves in the third person. They say things like, "I am glad you asked John Jones that question, and John Jones is ready to answer it." One day, I don't remember when it was, I found to my horror that I was referring to the column in the third person. I noticed a tendency for the column to be late for work. Worse, the column had developed a quality of complaint. It was a bit dull-eyed and not with it. So last winter I took the column to a clinic for a check-up.

The doctor turned out to be a friendly sort. "Well, now, this is a new one," he said. "I've never examined a column before. We've had frustrated housewives, neurotic salesmen, paranoid politicians, many cases of hypochondria. But never a rundown column." Next he pulled out a stethoscope and began listening. While he listened, he riffled through a pamphlet titled, *A Physician's Profitable Guide to the Money Market.* "Have to keep up on these things," he said. He listened to the stethoscope some more, then pronounced:

"Not a strong heart beat, but nothing to worry about. Comes with the aging process. How old is this column, anyway? Fifteen years? Twenty years? No matter. Often the aging process is more psychological than chronological. In the geriatric columns, I'd guess there's a tendency to repeat things. For example, I notice that this column begins a lot of paragraphs with the phrase, 'All in all.' Quite a few 'howevers' and 'meanwhiles' and 'on the other hands' in it. It also seems to have problems with transitions. We might call it a mild form of writing constipation. By the way, has it ever tried 'by the way' to start a sentence? That's a help sometimes."

A nurse came in and extracted a sample of the column's blood. The doctor went on probing. "I-I-I-I," he repeated, adding cheerfully: "No, I am not stuttering, just counting the number of 'I's in the column. Definitely too high an 'I' count. Instead of using 'I' so much, a healthy column should use 'we' now and then, or even 'one.' One shouldn't use too many 'I's now, should we?" he added, chuckling at his little joke.

While we waited for the column's blood analysis, the doctor doodled some dollar signs on a pad. "Damn shame," he muttered. "People have no idea how Medicare has fouled up our profession. Somebody ought to write a column about it." The nurse returned with the blood analysis. He studied the report, checked a biopsy of one paragraph, then announced: "Nothing terminal. Just an over-production of geriatrically-induced cliches, part of the aging process. A bit flabby, due to an underproduction of ideas. Blood count shows too many weak adverbs. Better cut down on commas, too. One shouldn't use too many commas, should one? That will be $250, please. Sorry to say that columns are not covered by Blue Cross."

So I took the column back down to the *P-I* and laid it on the editor's desk. "Here it is; I don't want it anymore. It has too much mileage on it and I would like to give it back to you and go do something else." Then I went off to Mexico, the way you do when you get a quickie divorce, and gave some thought to the future with no column for companionship. It felt wonderful. I also thought a lot about other people with columns inside them, having to disgorge these curious epistles day after day. The good ones endure. They go right on, hitting between guard and tackle every day, no matter how lousy they feel.

I once worked for a man named Royal Brougham, who for time and distance and endurance, was the Eighth Wonder of the World. He was in the newspaper business for sixty-eight years, most of them as a sports columnist, and it added up to thousands of columns, millions of words, written over an incredible span of time without interruption. He often wrote against a backdrop of pain and private sorrow. I remember seeing him double over his typewriter in physical anguish—a painful affliction of shingles—yet somehow he would rally to concentrate again.

Royal's old Underwood typewriter was battered and worn.

From many years of use, the keys were slicked down to bare metal; the painted letters had disappeared so that each key was bright, shiny—and blank. Also worn down to the metal was one spot in front of the space bar, a small area which Royal nervously rapped with the side of his balled-up fist as he strained for just the right word or phrase, a sentence with punch in it to quicken the beat of a story. He outlasted nine publishers at the *P–I* and perhaps a dozen editors with more rank than his, but he stayed too long.

In his later years he was a semi-invalid, shuffling along with a cane, his eyes sometimes vacant, his thoughts too much on the past. He never was good at remembering names but now, it seemed, even old acquaintances were met with, "Hi, fella." He became the object of private, patronizing remarks, the unknowing victim of amused tolerance. I used to hear some cruel jests about him and I was always sorry I didn't speak up and say, "You poor kid, you should have known him then. You couldn't carry his typewriter on the best day you ever saw." But I never said it, and I am sorry.

When he was at the top of his game he had the surest instinct for a story of any man I ever knew. He had an uncanny sense for what quickened a reader's interest, for what held a reader and brought him back day after day. This transcended Royal's faulty punctuation, his occasionally atrocious rationalization, and his frequent misspellings. Once when I corrected him on some minor grammatical error, he looked up and replied, somewhat pensively: "Thanks, kid, but you had a better education than I did. Nobody ever taught me these things."

His readers—at least the more erudite ones—who raged over his syntax and homilies did not see the irony. The irony was that Royal brought them to gaff. They were hooked on him because he had, as I said, that rare quality few writers have, the gift to excite and maintain the reader's interest. At his best, a period which roughly spanned the twenty years from 1935 to 1955, Royal Brougham's fan mail surpassed that of all other *P-I* writers combined.

His popularity brought power, but he used it cautiously. He saved his big guns for causes he believed in. "People forget," a former colleague of Royal's once said, "that he was once one of the most influential men in this state. Not just in sports but in any field. When he crooked a finger at them, they came like good boys." It was that power, used judiciously, that made it possible for him to raise enormous sums of money for charities. He put the *P-I* heavily into promotions and made the paper a profit in doing so. During World War II he raised more than $250,000 for servicemen's recreation. He cajoled and shamed the citizens of Seattle into desegregating public golf courses and bowling alleys and he chided the University of Washington for not recruiting good local black athletes. His power also translated into a better break for Japanese-Americans when World War II ended. He demanded "living memorials" in the form of playfields dedicated to the military dead, "instead of a statue of some old geezer sitting on an iron horse."

For years his column was called "The Morning After," but as somebody noted, "Royal never had one." A deeply religious man who taught Sunday school, he didn't smoke or drink, although he could eat enough at one sitting to feed a small elementary class. He had a true need for recognition that sprang from a genuine sense of insecurity. Thus his self-advertisements, both in and outside his column, were sometimes an embarrassment. But most of his quiet deeds of compassion and generosity went unrecorded. In the bottom of the Depression, when the order came out from the Hearst office in New York that low salaries had to be cut even lower—that a guy making $12.50 a week would now make $10.00—the cuts never hit Royal's sports department. He added up the cruel slashes in sports department paychecks and ordered them taken out of his own salary. It was years before anyone knew of that. And God knows how many students he helped, the jobs he got for ex-athletes, how many kids he helped through school, or the bucks he slipped to busted-down fighters.

The office he reigned over was an incredible gaggle of characters: half-illiterate copy boys, drop-in drunks, pastors, priests, politicians, athletes, gamblers, pimps and promoters. The man who never drank had a strange attraction for boozers, especially Joe Ryan, the self-styled "mayor of Bothell," who staggered in regularly to disrupt Royal's concentration. At one point Joe, perhaps moved by guilt, threw a big party for Brougham. In honor of the occasion— and the guest of honor—Joe stayed sober.

When Brougham was made sports editor in 1919, he did not forget his predecessor, Portus Baxter. He saw to it that Baxter would be paid a small sum as an adviser to the department, that he would write an old-timer's column. To the end of Baxter's life, Royal saw to his welfare. He was thunderstruck (along with everyone else) to learn that Portus, far from being almost penniless, had willed him more than $400,000 in blue-chip stocks. Royal used this windfall to set up a foundation which has helped more than three hundred kids of all races to attend college.

When the end came they had to cart him out of a press box. He collapsed in the Kingdome and died a few hours later in a hospital. It did not go unremarked that "Royal was a newspaperman to the end—he died on his own paper's edition time."

Royal's column was folksy and often corny. His blatant self-promotion, his simplistic platitudes, his contrived "your old neighbor" folksiness, could make one cringe at times. What matter? When I think of Royal's idiosyncrasies, I remember the story, perhaps apocryphal, of how Glenn Davis, the great Army halfback, broke away for an eighty-five yard touchdown run in his first practice game as a professional. When he came back to the bench, an assistant coach counseled Davis: "A good run, but you should have cut back earlier to get into our blocking pattern. You ran right over one blocker, and when you passed the line of scrimmage you held the ball too loose in the wrong arm." Davis listened politely and said, "How was it for distance?"

Royal Brougham went the distance.

How do you write a column? How the hell should I know? I'm not sure what a column really is. But since we have so many sex therapy experts who are eager (for a fee) to teach us how to copulate skillfully, someday we may get word therapists who can tell young geniuses how to achieve orgasms with the reader. I only know that columnists come in all shapes, sizes and conditions of literacy.

In the dot-dot-dot league, Herb Caen, of the *San Francisco Chronicle*, is in a class by himself. The three-dot columnist, best exemplified by the late Walter Winchell and his pale New York imitators, is an artist of a curious kind. Caen is far better at it than Winchell ever was, even in Winchell's best years. These "boiler plate" columns—the rivets are the three dots that separate each item—require the ability to impart (often with word coinage) newsy or humorous sentences into a minimum of space for each single item. In addition to being a master of this form, Caen also is a fine essayist, whose single-theme columns have been frequently published in book form. Above all, he is a digger and a reporter. Not long ago, Ben Bagdikian, a journalism critic on the University of California faculty, paid this tribute to Herb:

"Almost every day he has items that ought to be run at length as news, sometimes on page one. He has consistent wit and serious social values. He communicates the atmosphere of the city as no one else does."

Red Smith wrote slowly, painfully; this master at sports page composition once said that writing a column was like pricking a vein so that words came out, "like little drops of blood." Westbrook Pegler, the old curmudgeon, is said to have worked six or eight hours daily over his venomous prose. In a Philadelphia press box I once sat behind Bob Considine, one of the Hearst aces. While I labored over a game story, I looked up and noticed Considine passing little slips of paper, each with a single sentence, to the telegrapher at his elbow. He would type on a slip, pass it over, and go on to the next. I was astonished to find that Considine already had written his game story (the one I still labored on) and was now writing his column. Both his game story (a world series) and his column were written in about an hour.

Another great of the column racket was Heywood Broun. It is said that Broun, who loved to drink gin and play poker, would abruptly excuse himself for a few hands, leave the room and return in about thirty minutes. His column was done for the day. Georg Meyers, the *Seattle Times'* highly literate wordsmith, does his work briskly and rarely gets hung up by a difficult search for a word or phrase. Georg is a meticulous reporter, who absorbs things rapidly and does his homework, so that the actual writing seems to come easily.

Steve Rudman, a fine young columnist on the *P-I*, labors carefully over his stuff. You can usually find him in the company lunch room, alone in a corner, working up a rough draft in longhand; after an hour or so of this, he returns to the office to polish the final draft on a word processor.

Jim Murray, the celebrated sports columnist of the *Los Angeles Times*, is one who wastes no time. Murray's column frequently is a stream of one-liners that would make a Hollywood gag writer envious. But his concentration is consuming. A story is told of Murray covering the Muhammad Ali–George Foreman fight in Zaire. At ringside were dozens of electrical cords hooked up to television equipment and ring lights. A sudden torrential downpour washed over the press seats and water cascaded in and around the ring. While other writers scurried for safety, fearing imminent electrocution, Murray, up to his ankles in water and live cords, calmly went on with a stream of catchy one-liners to describe the fight.

Ed Donohoe, that once bibulous designer of insults and catch-names, labors hard on his column in the *Washington Teamster*. "There's always a lotta wrenching and false starts, but once you get it going it's not bad," he says. Henry Gay, writing in his own weekly *Shelton–Mason County Journal*, may well be the best (and most savage) satirist writing for newspapers today. Henry's columns, when not satirical, can be biting, sarcastic, broadly humorous and, of course, cruel. Gay's work has developed a devoted cult of readers, and his column, emanating out of Shelton, is syndicated in fifteen Northwest newspapers.

Many columnists, when actually experiencing literary birth pangs, inspire in the observer a mixture of wonder, pity and awe. A close look at Henry Gay, operating in a fantastically cluttered and irreverently festooned office, is provided by one of his former "interns" on the *Shelton–Mason County Journal*, a young man named John Maxim, Jr. Maxim, who spent a summer working for Henry, gives us a priceless glimpse of genius unfettered:

"The halls will echo with the sound of hysterical laughter. If you run down to his office and peer in, you will see Henry sitting at his typewriter, hands clutching his stomach, tears streaming down his cheeks, legs kicking, feet stomping and great gobs of laughter gasping from his chest. In a minute he regains his composure, puts his glasses (steel-rimmed half glasses) into place, scoots back up to his typewriter and resumes typing. When he says he writes for himself, you can believe it."

The best pure writer of humor this area ever produced was Doug Welch. I was always amazed at the slavish devotion of Welch fans; they were like addicts constantly in need of another Welch fix. His columns, called "The Squirrel Cage," were edited into two books by his widow Ruth, and they sold by the thousands. In describing Doug Welch—and literally hundreds have asked me what he was like—it would be foolish and dishonest to describe him as everybody's favorite uncle. It was a mistaken impression many people had of him. In print he portrayed himself as an amiable, ingenuous middle-class burgher. His columns made him seem completely at home with the people who populated what he called "my kooky neighborhood."

Welch was a sophisticated man, a serious, introspective fellow, widely read and not freely gregarious. He could be imperious at times and even resembled the actor, Sidney Greenstreet, in manner and bearing. At times he was open and friendly; he enjoyed a well-told joke, provided it carried a subtle point. He could be friendly, but he preferred privacy, or his own carefully-selected circle of friends. Welch was a model train buff. He would work off his day's writing trance by retiring to his basement, where he donned an engineer's cap, and ran his HO-gauge rail system. He told me this cut down on his evening consumption of martinis.

Welch was a writer of pure humor, some of the best humor America has produced. And people who write with this rare, fragile gift, who fashion it carefully, are somehow different from thee and me. Their world is in the mind, as everyone else's world is, of course, but people like Doug Welch have a peculiar vision of things. They see what you and I see, the foibles, pomposity, conformity, fads and absurdities all around, but they see it in a curiously skewed way. Though Welch seemed like one of us, he was recording what he saw as a spy in another country.

So in his feature writing days we got some hilarious stuff about solemn goings-on in this city, such as his famous "Park Board Reports" and his zany portrayals of city hall, one-way streets, and archaic booze laws. Later, as a columnist, he created broad spoofs of real characters such as Honest Al the Used Car Dealer, who invented his own religion, the Druids, in order to sell more cars. He gave us the beautiful Widow, that perennial threat to women in any neighborhood, and Mr. McMurty, the retired banker, "who only goes downtown to keep his hand in and foreclose a mortgage or two."

Welch had true star status at the paper, which meant he could come and go at will and work where he pleased. But he usually preferred to work at a desk in the city room with its clatter, noise and interruptions. He would answer the random phone calls that came in and he fended off his share of drunks and cranks. Once, when a lady called to report that her pet goose had laid what she believed to be a world record sized egg, Welch entered into the spirit of verification.

"How did you measure your goose's egg?" Welch inquired. "With your sewing tape measure? I'm afraid, madam, that no egg can be officially measured with only a tape measure. Do you have some calipers?" She didn't have any calipers, so Welch counseled her. "Go to the hardware store and buy some calipers. Only then can we tell if your egg is of world record size." A couple of hours later the woman called again. Yes, she had some calipers. "Fine, now measure your goose's egg carefully and report back to me. Meanwhile, I will check the record for goose eggs."

In due time the lady called back. "I'm sorry, madam," soothed Welch, "but I have not had time to check the goose egg record. You have measured yours? I'm afraid, madam, that you will need witnesses. Go and round up several of your neighbors who can testify to the dimensions when you measure your goose egg."

This went on for several more phone calls before Welch was forced to break the bad news. "I'm sorry, madam, but a check of our library shows that your goose egg falls somewhat short of a world record for size. If your goose lays another large egg be sure and call me back."

Between phone calls about goose eggs, Welch had pounded out another classic.

They come in all sizes and shapes. Johnny Reddin, a resolute reporter who loved to profile ordinary people in his *Seattle Times* column, was a short, square, ebullient fellow. While many columnists retreat into privacy, Reddin loved crowds and parties and all kinds of people. He was the antithesis of the *Times'* image of stately conservatism and decorum. It was not unusual to find Reddin poking his forefinger into the chest of a city official (even the mayor or police chief) delivering in machine-gun sentences his view of how the city should be run. But if Reddin had an enemy in this city, I have not heard of him.

Johnny Reddin covered all kinds of stories—robberies, fires, waterfront fights, police battles and water shutoffs—before he became one of Seattle's best-loved chroniclers of people and events. As a police reporter he frequently napped on a cot in the press room after a hard night of chasing around with cops, topped off by a session in a handy after-hours joint. Many newsies have their favorite Reddin stories, but my own concerns the occasion some years ago when the *Seattle Times* was shut down by a strike, the announcement coming during a Reddin nap in the press room.

A police sergeant, hearing the news that the strike was, indeed, underway, came in and shook Reddin awake. "John, wake up," he said, rousing our hero. "You gotta know this, your paper's on strike." Reddin, half awake, waved the cop off grumpily. "Yeah, I know, I know, this thing has been coming on for some time."

"What're you striking for?" asked the cop. Reddin collapsed blissfully back on the cot to resume his nap. "Better working conditions," he said.

To say anything about Leroy Ostransky is not to say enough, since he is a massive talent in many fields. How does he excel? Let me count the ways: raconteur, composer, teacher, trencherman, writer and columnist (these last two terms are not mutually exclusive). Until he retired two years ago, Ostransky was composer-in-residence and professor of music at the University of Puget Sound, but do not let these lofty titles confuse you. Leroy is about as elitist as an old shoe. He was born in Brooklyn and his father, whom he loved, "was a bootlegger, racketeer and mobster." It should be added at this point that Leroy likes to exaggerate. His own

Brooklynese, clear, precise and strong, has resisted modification in the thirty-seven years he has lived in Tacoma. How he got there may be instructive.

During World War II, Leroy found himself plucked off the streets of Brooklyn, where he once delivered bathtub gin to his father's speakeasy. He was sent to Fort Lewis for army training. After five months at Fort Lewis, he fell in love with the Northwest, but was headed back on furlough for a visit to his Brooklyn turf. On the train he met a tough-looking army sergeant whose chest was a galaxy of battle ribbons, signifying action in Europe, Africa and such bloody Pacific campaigns as Tarawa, Iwo Jima and Guadalcanal.

Tarawa! Iwo Jima! The very names, locales of great American heroism, put Leroy's own citation, "The American Theatre Ribbon," in a class with the Good Housekeeping Seal of Approval. Leroy struck up a hesitant conversation with the battle-starred sergeant. He explained how he was going home to Brooklyn, how his principal hazardous combat duty thus far consisted of crossing a Tacoma street at rush hour. He would, Leroy explained, be visiting his old buddies in Brooklyn saloons. These civilians would no doubt buy him drinks. But sooner or later, he said, they would ask him what his single decoration, "American Theatre," meant. The veteran of Iwo Jima and Tarawa listened sympathetically.

"Since you got drafted," asked the sergeant, "where have you been?" Leroy said he had been stationed near Tacoma. The sergeant brightened. "Tell you what, kid," said the veteran of Tarawa, "when you go back to Brooklyn, go into a saloon and sit by yourself. When a civilian comes up and offers to buy you a drink, he'll look at your ribbon. Then he'll say, 'Where you been, soldier?' You just say, 'Tacoma.'

And he'll say, 'Tacoma, where's that?' You just shake your head as though it was too painful to remember. Then you say, 'Tacoma. I don't want to talk about it.' "

Leroy went back to Tacoma, and except for an occasional visit to Brooklyn or Europe, he has been there ever since. He even wrote a book about his adopted city called, *How to Live in Tacoma and Like It*. He stayed there, studied, got his Ph.D., and has published four symphonies. His book, *The Anatomy of Jazz*, is now in its umpteenth printing and is considered the definitive work on jazz. I first worked with Leroy on the weekly *Argus* back in 1963 and used to shiver with joy when his columns came in for editing. They rarely needed so much as a comma, and they were a joy to read. For years, I tried to get the Big Thinkers at the *P–I* to hire this man with the wit and erudition of a Benchley, but having failed at that, I'm happy to say that Leroy has for years written a weekly column for the *Tacoma News Tribune*.

I have heard through friendly sources that Leroy's capacity for drink and provender has abated somewhat with the years. But he still can sit at a piano, composing extemporaneously, and loudly sing "lyrics" from the ad copy in a Sears catalogue. And mine eyes have seen the glory. One historic day I met Leroy for breakfast at nine-thirty, during which he consumed a breakfast steak, two eggs, hash browns, much toast and jam. As we left the restaurant, Leroy checked his watch. "It's now almost eleven-thirty," he said. "Where are we having lunch?" We walked a few blocks to Rosellini's Four-10, where Leroy ordered three double vodkas with soda on the side. "Now bring me," he said to the waiter, "a large plate of spaghetti." We talked a while longer and Leroy signaled the waiter again. "Bring me another plate of spaghetti." When this plate had been devoured with an appropriate loaf of French bread, he said, "Now bring the dessert cart."

Leroy surveyed the dessert cart the way a co-pilot checks out an airplane before takeoff. Then he said, "Take it away. I could eat everything on it but I've got to cut down."

Tall and imposing, gargantuan in talent, Leroy cuts a huge figure in our newspapering scene. But mere physical dimensions are meaningless, and columnists come in strange packages. Nard Jones was a short man, rather stout, somewhat jowly in the cheeks, and bald. A small mustache gave him a puckish, cherubic appearance. Although he was conservative politically and in his social values as well, underneath there always seemed to lurk the soul of a revolutionary, dedicated to overthrowing the solemnity and alleged sanity of the workaday world.

There was an enchanting zaniness in the complex person who was Nard Jones. There are memories of his flashing wit, his ecstatic grasp of the ridiculous, his hilarious self-mocking charades. Nard Jones was a columnist. He was any kind of writer you could name. He wrote many columns in his career, but he also wrote magazine stories and editorials and I suspect he could have written some fine poetry had he wished. In all he wrote sixteen books and countless articles, essays and reviews.

His madness was compulsively contrived, for Nard was often tortured and afraid. He had a constant problem with booze and he once told me, "I was forty years old before I discovered that alcohol didn't flow in a turkey's veins on Thanksgiving." On any given morning he would march into the P–I's newsroom and call out in a loud voice, "Who do we hate today?" That was his revolt against a solemn editorial demeanor. To relieve tedium he once buried himself in a huge canvas-sided pickup cart and prevailed on a copy boy to wheel him up to Doug Welch's desk. There, with a maniacal cry, he popped out and dumped a load of teletype tape over Welch's head. On another occasion he let out an insane shriek, dashed across the room to a window and began throwing piles of useless paper out on the street.

He was a consummate actor, who could, with appropriate charades, collapse a listener with some old chestnut of a joke. "It is a sample," he would explain, "of my Umatilla County humor."

An old friend of Nard's was Oscar Gowing, of Bellevue, who can regale one with Jones anecdotes. Oscar related a time when he was parked at a downtown Bellevue service station during a severe rain storm. "One man was ahead of me in the pump stand and there was a lady parked at the other side of the pump. It had been raining hard and steadily for almost two weeks with scarcely a letup. Nard Jones drove into the station in his little sports car and spotted me. Pretending not to know me, he shouted to everyone within hearing distance, 'Run for your lives! The Clyde Hill Dam has broken. Not a moment to lose, get out of here!' Then he went racing off, his horn blaring. The terrified lady rolled up her windows and flooded her engine in a frantic effort to drive out. The man in front of me yelled out his window to the station operator, 'Shut down the station and call the fire department!'

"As for me, I just sat there, trying to remember where the Clyde Hill Dam was located. Then I knew why I couldn't remember. We'd all been had by Nard Jones."

His judgment of other people's work was keen. Many a time he bailed out other writers—I was one of the lucky ones—with a detached, sensitive evaluation of their work. He read copy carefully, because he respected other writers' feelings, and he went out of his way, on dozens of occasions, to encourage young and eager talents. If he had an editorial hero, it probably was the late Miller Freeman, for whose advertising publications Nard worked in his early years of journalism. But even Freeman, a hard taskmaster, did not escape Nard's barbed humor. From Europe Nard cabled Freeman, "I've seen the salt mines in Siberia, and frankly I prefer them."

A friend once said that Nard Jones "was almost too fragile for work on a newspaper." This may be so. But he produced, as I say, fine columns, reviews and essays. One of his early novels, *Swift Flows the River*, was one of the first books out of Seattle to hit the best-seller lists. *The Great Command,* an historical study of Marcus Whitman, the celebrated Northwest pioneer, sold well and was widely acclaimed. Nard Jones, it seemed to me, never was able to come to terms with a basic contradiction within himself. He admired establishment figures, the businessmen of success and power, but this he could not reconcile with his own natural skepticism—a necessary quality in any good writer.

He enjoyed being taken to the Rainier Club or the University Club, but his own turf was the College Club, somewhat lower in Seattle's clubbish pecking order. Even here he could not totally abide the necessary decorum. I am indebted to Tommy Todd, the local attorney, for passing on an example of Nard's humor—a letter he once wrote to the College Club's Board of Trustees, protesting the price of drinks. The letter was written in 1939, so the prices are dated, but the message is not.

"Gentlemen," he wrote, "I wish to protest violently against the rise in liquor prices in the College Club bar. It seems to me that thirty cents for a drink is prohibitive. As I sit here writing I am enjoying a highball made with Mono-gram Rye. I calculate that this drink cost eleven cents. If I were purchasing it instead of mixing my own, I would con-sider fifteen cents a very fair price.

"To prove my point I am going to mix another one. I find that it takes about two minutes. Also as an experiment I take one straight and find that this takes approximately a half minute. Yet you already charge as mush for the highball as you do for the straight drink.

"I wish to say that the hole matter is an outrage and would be resented by anny fair-minded Ammerican in his right mine. &&-### Liquor was given back to the peoples as one of their rights and now you are trying to take it away from them by making the $$$$ prohibitionary.

"I am not signing my name as there is alwys those 3who think that a gyu who takes a drink doessn't have possession of his $5999& reasonable facilities. thassa damlie and I make better drinks right at homme and not pay so %$$### mcuh. (signed) Outranged memmer."

Nard edited a boating magazine and wrote columns about boats and he owned one himself. But such was his deep sus-picion of the internal combustion engine that he rarely used it. "I always had that feeling of sheer terror when I pushed the starter button. Each time I was convinced it would blow up." He hated and feared freeways, but he drove a tiny Triumph through the terrifying traffic, wearing a Cossack hat, perhaps another revolt against capitalist authority and its works.

One of my last memories of Nard Jones was stopping by his office, expecting some zany caper, joke or charade. Instead I found him in a pensive mood. I sat there for a while in the silence and finally Nard looked up and said, "Isn't it a shame that after men get married, the flower shops are always on the other side of the street?''

┌─────────┐
│   │
│   3   │
│   │
└─────────┘

Bloodless Bureaucracy

"Parody is good for the soul," John Lardner once told me, and he would know, since the son of Ring Lardner wrote some of the deadliest parodies ever to appear in print. His high mark, I always thought, was a parody he did of Jack Paar, the one-time television night show host, whose shallow intellect and petulant ego made a perfect target for the Lardner take-off on his style. Another classic of this difficult genre was Wolcott Gibbs' famous profile of *Time*, written entirely in the pretentious, convoluted, bassackwards style which marked that Henry Luce publication in the 1930s and 1940s. I tried many times to cleanse my own soul with parody but results were mostly negative; readers yawned, the soul remained uncleansed.

Aside from the writer's talent, a good parody requires that the average reader knows what the devil is being parodied. It does no good to parody a person, or a book, or a television show, if few people know much about them. About the only passable one I ever did centered on the old Seattle City Council of the late fifties and early to mid-sixties.

For the most part these council members were older folks, long past any prime they may have had. A number of them came to city government as acceptable packages, delivered and guaranteed by the Rotary, Kiwanis, Elks, Lions, Optimists, Moose and various other booster groups and commercial clubs that controlled Seattle in those years. They bore names like Myrtle Edwards, Clarence Massart, Ted Best, Ed Riley, Paul Alexander, Floyd Miller, Ray Eckmann, Dorm Braman (who later became mayor) and "Streetcar Charlie" Carroll, the latter being the only one with more color than the average glass of water.

Taken singly, they were decent, upstanding people. Put together as a governing body of Seattle they and their predecessors, cast in a similar mold, had a bad effect on each other, like too many maple bars stuck together in a single paper bag; they glued themselves into a state of grim, unanimous inaction, sensitive only to spurious issues, galvanized only by dog-leash laws and unenforced anti-noise ordinances. They were the kind of people who gave Seattle such visual delights as the Alaskan Way Viaduct and the architectural triumph of the Public Safety Building.

In the late 1930s, the Cincinnatus reform movement did great things by ridding the city of corrupt politicians and cops. Another reform movement in the 1960s called CHECC, for Choose an Effective City Council, was not formed necessarily to save the city from corruption; it was trying to save it from atrophy. That CHECC's leaders succeeded in their efforts at resuscitation is a civic blessing, since the city gained, throughout the difficult period of the late 1960s and the 1970s, a collection of younger and more progressive leaders.

But the mossback city government of those long gone years could be a columnist's smorgasbord. One could rant, rave, carp and poke fun at the do-nothing city fathers. Since they rarely did much else, they made news out of trivia—dog licensing, dirty movies, and, God bless them all, bloodless bullfighting. I forget the details, but a couple of promoters came to Seattle with the idea of putting on bullfights which would not include banderillas, pics or any other bloodletting equipment that might offend Seattle's overwhelming Anglo-Saxon sensitivity.

Nevertheless, the inescapable designation, "bullfighting," caused a predictable howl among the citizenry. The promoters insisted that bloodless bullfighting was well-received elsewhere. Intelligent men would have passed or rejected the promoters' request in five minutes, but these fusty do-nothings let a modest proposal blow up into a civic storm. The whole thing seems unreal now (as it did then) but the city council actually agreed to attend the film screening of a bloodless bullfight in order to reach its august decision.

Mike Conant, currently the *P-I*'s estimable book editor, was then covering city hall. He called me to confirm that, indeed, five grown men, five of the nine city council members, would take the afternoon off to watch a movie of bloodless bullfighting. Mike said they would watch the screening at KING-TV, then under the leadership of Stimson Bullitt. That is how I got off the only halfway decent parody I ever wrote. Admirers of the late Mr. Ernest Hemingway may not be amused:

"Are they going to let us see the bulls, Papa?" she asked, and he respected her for it, loving the clean pure lines of her syntax, remembering also the cool, sunlit mornings, sorry now that she was troubled by the town burghers who were against the bulls. The Humane Society too, he thought, remembering truly, and the dried-up Garden Clubs breaking the spirit of Pamplona. "We'll see, Little Rabbit," Papa said, shifting his weight off the old wound, remembering Caporetto, and feeling the deep cavity in his tooth, the old deep, painful wound suffered at the last Battle of Fluoridation.

"This is Seattle, Little Rabbit," he said, getting it down truly. "The blood flows thin here, not like Pamplona, where the bulls were brave and ran in the streets, when there was none of this obscenity corruption of trimming the horns and padding the hump where the kill is made."

Papa paid his own check and left her there, feeling unfulfilled about the bulls. This morning he did not have his usual absinthe at Dag's, but moved on down Aurora, moving across the street and into the screening room. "I still cross good," he thought, shifting his wineskin as he passed the office of Señor Stimson Bullitt, feeling the earth move but not being afraid.

Papa entered the screening room and he could see them there in the dark, and he remembered them truly. "The bloodless ones," he thought, again remembering the old men truly: Massart, Eckmann, Best, Riley, Alexander, noting that Mrs. Edwards was not there. Papa smiled his old death smile. "I must get it down truly, the way it really happened," he said to himself, "cutting out the bad parts, writing truly and with bravery so that it will last and not go bad before Seafair."

He studied their faces, looking for the familiar signs of fear, thinking back on the old battles he had written truly about, the Ravenna Cave-In, the Topless Revolution, the Retreat from Sapro, the bitter skirmishes of the Dog Leash Law. Still smiling the old death smile, but revealing nothing, Papa measured their bravery in the old campaigns, knowing that they guarded their flanks with excellence, but remembering how they panicked, running lumpily away when divisions of the PTA were brought up, knowing they could not be trusted when confronted by the Goodness Brigade.

Remembering truly, he compared them with El Sordo on the hilltop, Señor Rinaldi, Lieutenant Henry, and Robert Jordan, with Jake Barnes and even Pablo. He wished Mrs. Edwards had come to this obscenity screening so he could compare her with Pilar. "Old men," he thought, "you should have been at Caporetto where you would have learned how we retreated good."

Papa watched their faces closely as the screening began, the screening of the bloodless bullfight, and suddenly he remembered the Little Rabbit, whom he had left in the cafe an hour before, wondering if she had remembered that it was Dutch treat. "If it comes to that," he thought, "yes, if it comes to that. She can wash dishes. She washes good dishes."

The bloodless bullfight came on the screen, and Papa got that old, bad sick feeling when the matador turned the cape too tight, bringing the bull around hard, abusing its bravery. He was a small bull, Papa noted, truly a nineteen-cent hamburger bull, with his horns shaved to please the matador, not bloodied by the picador, getting none of the banderillas. Not like the uncertain older bulls favored by Belmonte and Joselito. And the matador, he thought. Yes, the matador. Well, now the matador. He decided, feeling again the old dead sickness inside, that the matador belonged with the Seafair Pirates. "Or washing dishes," he said, without pity.

Papa studied the faces of the old men in the reflected light of the screen. He shifted his weight off the old wound, remembering how it was in the rain at Caporetto, using his pencil with grace and bravery, getting it all down the way it really happened, writing his notes truly and regretting that he had to do journalism until his next movie sale. "This and that for the town majors," he thought, eyeing their bloodless faces, not liking their looks in the dim light of Señor Bullitt's screening room. "I obscenity in the milk of thy city charter," he said, not saying it aloud because he did not wish to provoke. "I do not provoke," he thought, "but we retreated good at Caporetto."

And now, remembering that El Sordo was very brave, that he took fellow voyagers with him, Papa decided to make his stand on the hilltop, aware that the enemy would be back now that the bullfight had ended, knowing the enemy would return with new forces, the forces of goodness, the obscenity dry lifeless ones, beautifully detached and cruel as they break you. Papa left the screening room, feeling the tension, the dry throat, but not showing fear as he made his way to Capitol Hill, the high ground, his back to the phone booth where he set up his position to await the attack from city hall.

He tried not to think of the Little Rabbit washing dishes. He used the wineskin sparingly as he waited, guarding his position carefully, remembering all the old, lost battles clearly, determined to get this one down the way it really happened. "At least I did not provoke," he said, thinking of the dry deadly faces of the town burghers. The phone rang and it was Mike, doing reconnaissance behind enemy lines at city hall. True, brave and reliable Mike Conant, who would not break under the torture of town meetings. Mike spoke warmly and truly. "Papa," he said, "they voted for the bulls, Papa. You hear me truly, Papa? We get the bulls at Seattle Center."

"Our luck, she is running good," said Papa, tasting the good warm feeling of the wine from the goatskin. "If we win here, we can win everywhere."

For the life of me, I can't remember if we ever really had a bloodless bullfight in Seattle. The whole thing is too tedious to look up. Even at this distance, I obscenity in the milk of thy city charter.

4

Blithe Spirits

John Kenneth Galbraith, the noted economist-journalist, once said, "Anyone who reads in a compulsive way should be allowed one sordid aberration—an interest in pornography, abnormal psychology, or the chronicles of professional basketball." My own aberration is the company of what some editorial towers would regard as the lowlifes of journalism. I refer, of course, to the press agents, or as they are sometimes derisively called, "flacks." I have always had trouble making the distinction between a press agent who hustles space for a boxer, a ball club, a hotel, a restaurant or a church bazaar, and those who carry such lofty titles as "director of information" or "corporate counsel for public affairs." By any definition, no matter how many Brooks Brothers suits they wear, the latter are no better than the former—my friends, the flacks.

Consider if you will, that almost any news story emanating from Washington, D.C., is manipulated either by a corporation's "public relations counsel" or his equivalent at the Pentagon or any other large government bureaucracy. Any time you see a headline which says, "Reagan Presses for Arms Buildup," you can safely assume that some media manipulator, or a whole battery of them, is behind it. Even the president's wishes, as related to the news services, hence to newspapers across the country, are filtered through his public relations people, tailoring the prose and statements to his style. When you read that Puget Power, or Pacific Northwest Bell, is urging a rate increase, rest assured that a "media consultant," or a vice-president in charge of public information, is right there earning the dough that keeps up his dues in a country club.

The true press agent, or flack, differs only in the size of his clients, the thickness of his wallet, the quality of his Scotch, and the size of his office, if he even has one. The really good flacks can operate within a corporation (which they don't usually like) or hustle space for a circus or an ice show. The press agents I have known and kept company with are canny, conniving, funny, cynical, bold, outrageous, imaginative, undependable, and altogether wonderful. Alas, I fear they are on the endangered species list.

Because of their need to survive, many press agents have been forced to take steady jobs. They do this in order to pay their grocery bills and their bar bills, not necessarily in that order. You may have heard of the Skagit Belle. This was a paddle wheel curiosity that sank at Pier 54 and, weighted by litigation, stayed down for many months. Well, in the years I kept company with press agents, among us we drank enough Scotch to refloat the Skagit Belle.

It's also possible that you have heard of Ocean Shores, a property development which rests on a glorified sand spit just west of Grays Harbor. This sand spit was once just a sand spit, content with its lowly station. Now it is a rather famous community, and the reason it is a famous community is because a chap I know, Robert Narraganset Ward, made it that way. Bob Ward is a press agent who was hired by Bill MacPherson, the early developer of Ocean Shores, to help him sell property down there. If Mr. MacPherson had not had the foresight (and the courage) to give Bob Ward free rein with his creative talents, the world might never have heard of Cutliffe Sarkvogle and Ocean Shores would still be a sand spit.

Cutliffe Sarkvogle, according to Ward, was a freelance shellfish consultant. "He lives on a three-goat stump ranch at Elk Sign, which is a remote nook of Grays Harbor County," Ward would insist. Ward went on to recall that bears in Grays Harbor County came out of the woods to watch television through the window of Cutliffe Sarkvogle's shake-covered shack. One evening the bears became miffed because Cutliffe switched channels, thus depriving them of their favorite TV show, "Yogi Bear." The bears clawed the shakes off Sarkvogle's shack.

Ward then pointed out that more and more tourists drove to Ocean Shores in order to drink in its semi-pristine beauty. That is not an ill-chosen phrase, since for a long time the community's principal recreation was drinking. So Grays Harbor County Commissioners began to receive letters, urging them to build a "bear overpass" to protect residents on the busy Copalis Beach highway. These letters were all signed by Cutliffe Sarkvogle, a true friend of bears, even after the shingle-ripping incident.

Wire services, radio stations and newspapers made quite a fuss over Cutliffe Sarkvogle. Many of them tried to get private interviews with Sarkvogle, but Ward managed to fend them off, and Cutliffe eventually went back where he came from, not in a sheltered shack, but in the recesses of Mr. Ward's scheming imagination. Ward worked at Ocean Shores for twelve years and, as the clerk of the Ocean Shores Municipal Court, a nice lady named Helen Mayes explained it: "When Bob Ward left, so did Cutliffe. We miss them both."

George Vancouver, a British navy captain, charted most of the Washington coastline. On April 27, 1792, Captain Vancouver sailed past Ocean Shores. Most reputable historians are ignorant of this important date, but according to Bob Ward, whose own research is unassailable until other historians get around to disputing it, the date of April 27, 1792, was the day when Captain Vancouver sailed HMS *Discovery* past Ocean Shores without noticing it. Hence an Ocean Shores tradition, observed in several journals printed in English—the tradition of Undiscovery Day. Efforts to declare Undiscovery Day a state holiday have proved to be unsuccessful, which may yet turn into Unsuccessful Day.

When he worked at the *P–I* many years ago, Ward says he studied at the knee of a great circus press agent named Bouncing MacDougall. It is unclear why he was called "Bouncing," but Ward plainly admired MacDougall's flair for promoting circuses. Together they arranged for Bouncing MacDougall to bring a small elephant, name of Rosa, to the *P–I* newsroom for a purpose now lost in memory. Rosa and Bouncing MacDougall showed up but Ward forgot his appointment with Rosa, who scared everybody half to death as she lumbered through the newsroom. "I prudently stayed away for a couple of days when I learned what happened," Ward recalls. "It seemed that Rosa was not housebroken."

Press agentry, or hucksterism, as opposed to serious news coverage, was in Ward's blood. While still a reporter he invented a scheme to accompany a head of lettuce to Nome, Alaska, to dramatize the fact that fresh vegetables were now being flown in from the Lower 48. Upon arrival, Ward found himself in the middle of a party which, he discovered, was being held to celebrate the reopening of Nome's first whorehouse after World War II.

"Naturally, I had to give a speech," he says. "I told the townspeople that my chief, Mr. William Randolph Hearst himself, would editorially endorse this spendid example of Americanism and free enterprise, the stuff that made America great. I predicted that Nome's go-getter spirit would result in statehood for Alaska. I turned out to be right, but perhaps for the wrong reason."

Ward's free-flowing imagination has promoted such Seattle institutions as Dag's hamburgers and KOL radio, along with Tacoma's historic Winthrop Hotel. At the Winthrop he once threw a picnic in the lobby for the town's leading citizens, then released a story, printed prominently in Tacoma's only paper, denying a rumor that the name of the hotel might be changed. Ward's publicity handout proclaimed that the hotel owners, ever mindful of Tacoma's historical traditions, would stick with the proud name of Winthrop. Readers may have been puzzled by this announcement, Ward admits, "because somehow I forgot to spread the original rumor before issuing a denial."

As Ward's fame at putting obscure places on the map began to spread, he was summoned (for a fee) by a campground owner in Pend Oreille County, north of Spokane. Ward discovered that the campground consisted mainly of a general store, a gas station, a buffalo pen (one buffalo), a tavern and a nine-hole golf course. It was plain that people could scarcely be lured there for a bite of the Big Apple. But Ward discovered that the campground was located near the little town of Usk. He immediately launched the Usk Open Golf Tournament. Rules were designed for team play. Ward advertised the tournament as "Usk vs. Them," issuing T-shirts bearing the proud head of the campground's single buffalo. This was the Usk team. The team known as Them got a picture of the buffalo's other end.

I occasionally encounter my friend Ward, who comes to Seattle when he can. He suffered a stroke a few years back, which slowed him only temporarily, and he still works for the redoubtable Bill MacPherson, publicizing a lot-selling project near Bend, Oregon. His headquarters, he says, "are in Horny Hollow on Crooked River Ranch." The last time I saw him he came up to promote another of his classic sporting events, the May Mule Mile, which features mules running (or walking) uphill. He said that a local jogger measured the Mule Mile course and discovered it was missing a furlong. He thinks that is too bad, and he said he might call the *Louisville Courier-Journal* about it.

"They give the Mule Mile good publicity back there," he explained. "The first year I started the Mule Mile I called the *Louisville Courier-Journal* to find out when they ran the Kentucky Derby." I said that asking a Louisville paper for the date of the Kentucky Derby would be like calling the Vatican to find out the late J.C.'s birthday. Mr. Ward agreed. But he said he called the Louisville paper and assured them he wanted to check on the dates, "because we didn't want two big races going on the same day and competing for publicity. The *Courier-Journal* was quite nice about it," he added. "The editor was so pleased by my courtesy that he gave us a good story on the Mule Mile."

Ward may have been the most flamboyant, but he wasn't

the first press agent to pump up this region. Erastus Brainerd, an early newspaper editor in Seattle, is rightly canonized as the city's first great press agent. When gold was discovered in Alaska, Brainerd, a booster at heart, saw his chance. He cranked out reams of publicity on Seattle as the jumping-off place to riches; when he described the first ship coming back after the strike as being loaded with "a ton of gold," the city basked in its first taste of national publicity. Local historian Bill Speidel, himself no mean hand at press agentry, points out that Seattle has always thrived on the stuff of press agents. From the time the first settlers arrived, Speidel has said, the natives have scarcely stopped selling Seattle.

One of the more sterling fellows in the selling-of-Seattle dodge is an old friend, Guy Williams, a man who is very skilled at image-building. Guy is a tall, rugged looking, kindly man whose heritage goes back to the days he spent in logging camps. He is a scholarly type, very much a product of the Northwest, with a wildly funny sense of humor—and more importantly, a sense of proportion. It delights his often satirical view of things to concoct schemes to catch people's attention. Together with Ivar Haglund, the one-man clam cartel, Williams devised Haglund's Pacific Free-Style Amateur Clam-Eating Competition. Williams' satirical eye, noting that no such festival can do without a queen, devised the notion that this promotion would acquire a certain dignified sex appeal by having a beauty queen known as Miss Halibut Cheeks.

Williams has spent some fifty years as a huckster, although he, more than most, was able to slip into the more dignified and restrained role of a corporate media advisor. On the other side of the bargaining table, he joined with Jack Gordon in sprucing up the image of the Teamsters Union when Dave

Beck was a national power in the union ranks. It was Williams who had a large hand in developing Seafair and he claims to have learned much from the late Walter Van Camp, who was head of Seafair during that celebration's glory years in the fifties.

Not long ago Williams told *Seattle Times* reporter Frederick Case that the key role of a press agent is to "stimulate the munificence and kindness of the rich and powerful, to butter up egos and give out scrolls." Williams, because of his own detached, mocking sense of humor, made friends with dozens of key news people, notably Doug Welch, who had immense reportorial power when he worked at news and feature writing. A sort of floating Algonquin Table, which met mostly at a big table at the old Olympic Grill, was where a lot of promotional ideas got launched off a cocktail napkin. This group, which often included Welch, Williams and Gordon, and to a lesser extent the *P-I*'s inimitable feature writer, the late Jack Jarvis, hatched innumerable schemes to promote the city and its clients.

One of the group summed up these latter-day Algonquins for Case: "We used to get together for lunch and steal ideas from each other. We were a pretty raucous lot. I don't suppose the modern 'public relations counselors,' with their button-down oxford shirts, would even want to be in the same room with us."

Jack Gordon, who has now settled in as executive vice-president of the Washington State Restaurant and Hotel Association, was once a free-floating spirit of civic merchandising. Gordon acquired national attention by devising (along with one of Seattle's rare lively city council members, Al Rochester) the custom of greeting troopships during the Korean War. Gordon was not only a master salesman, he had few peers as a cheer-em-on master of ceremonies, and he turned the greeting of the troopships into a civic institution.

While also doing part-time publicity for Seattle University, Gordon in effect caught lightning in a bottle—and he knew what to do with it. In those early days of the 1950s, Seattle University basketball was about one step above the YMCA in quality. In order to get publicity—any publicity—for his team, Gordon would cover the game, keep statistics, then rush to the *Times* and *P-I* to hustle what space he could. Usually, if the department was short-handed, the sports desk would insist that Gordon write his own stories, since they weren't about to waste their own precious literary talent on a team of hamburgers playing strictly local opponents.

All that changed one winter with the arrival of a matched set of identical twins, Johnny and Eddie O'Brien, who towered a full five feet, nine inches tall. They were from South Amboy, New Jersey. To greet them on arrival was a flexible coaching genius named Horace Albert Brightman and several astonished Jesuit priests, at least one of whom expected the O'Briens' recruiter, whoever he was, to show up at confession and try to absolve his sin of bringing Seattle U two midgets to play basketball. But it was plain, to Brightman at least, that the two could play basketball with fervor, zip and dash. It took Brightman a year to make a revolutionary decision—that of putting Johnny O'Brien in the "pivot," or center position, a job usually reserved for young men bordering on giantism.

And it took Jack Gordon no time at all to realize that he had a press agent's dream. Johnny O'Brien, being fed passes by his identical twin brother Ed (they were almost indistinguishable then), began to run up some horrendous point totals. Thus Gordon began cranking out reams of publicity, full of colorful allusions to Seattle U's "little giant," and the feast was on. It hurt not at all that Johnny O scored forty-five points as Seattle U beat the famed Harlem Globetrotters, or that Seattle U, with John scoring some forty points, beat New York University in Madison Square Garden by the then unbelievable score of 102–101. Gordon no longer had to hurry into sports departments to write his own stories; he had to beat off sportswriters with a club.

The most improbable feat of all was that Johnny O'Brien eventually was named to a major college All-American team. While it is true that Johnny O had a spectacular talent for dropping balls through a hoop, it was Gordon, through imaginative exploitation, who built up the media pressure that made both O'Briens bywords among America's college basketball fans.

All this, in its own way, added up to the selling of Seattle. But much of this selling began virtually without a product, as was the case with Jim Faber, an imaginative ex-newsman, who became "PR director" for the Seattle World's Fair. This extravaganza, held in 1962, is now firmly embedded in our history. Business leaders have gone to their graves being canonized for their work in bringing the fair off, but it was Faber who had a large part in getting it started at all.

Jim is the closest thing we have here who can be typed as a "media consultant," and as he admits freely, "If you asked me to sell a basketball player or a clam-digging contest, I wouldn't know where to begin." But what he lent to the fair was a shrewd judgment of publicity values and a persuasive way of directing the unskilled Babbits involved in the fair's planning. Without him, some of their simplistic ideas might have got them laughed out of town.

Faber combined his common sense perspective with a

profitable instinct for bluffing. With no budget to speak of in those early days, he descended on Washington, D.C., and put up at a cheap hotel. Working in large part from an earlier friendship with Washington's powerful senator, Warren G. Magnuson, Faber cased the federal till for any spare change he could find. The fair had virtually no commitments from any large exhibitors, and when one federal bureaucrat asked Faber who the exhibitors would be, he obligingly came up with a list.

This list included such large companies as Pacific Northwest Bell, United States Steel and a couple of others. Their "commitment" to the fair consisted largely of a willingness to sell things once the fair got going. "This," said Mr. Faber, casually, "is a partial list." It is not recorded that the federal till immediately popped open, but with the help of Faber's low-key efforts in Washington, Magnuson was able to extract $15 million for the project.

It was Faber, on a visit to Paris, who trumped up publicity that France's famed luxury liner, the *Ile de France,* might come to Seattle to serve as a floating hotel. He was not remiss in hinting publicly that untold hordes of visitors would tax the city's limited rooming space. He also devised a contraption called the Atomic Countdown Chronometer. This marvel of technological science was slapped together by some local television engineers at Faber's request. "It resembled a big jukebox," he recalls now, "and its atomic power consisted of an electric cord plugged into an outlet."

Faber had learned that President Eisenhower was passing through Seattle. His Atomic Countdown Chronometer was designed to record the elapsed time until the World's Fair officially opened. He then shipped it out to meet Eisenhower's plane when the president landed at Boeing Field.

Mr. Eisenhower, carefully briefed in advance, obligingly pushed the countdown button and the whole absurd episode churned up international publicity for the fair.

Working on a less global scale is Jack Macdonald whose imagination has fertilized such promotions as a St. Patrick's Day "snake race," featuring a half-dozen rented boa constrictors and a tortoise-and-hare handicap race, the handicap being that the hare lost interest and refused to run. True to Aesopian folk wisdom, the tortoise came in first. Both of these events drew thousands of people and no doubt elevated Macdonald's then client, radio station KVI, a fraction of a point in listener ratings. Macdonald got radio promotion down to about as exact a science as it deserves to be. He wrote a handbook on radio promotions which sold briskly to small town stations all over America. One of his stunts may even have resulted in some social good.

Checking the statutes some years ago, Macdonald discovered that there were no restrictions whatever on the issuing of hunting licenses in Washington. This meant, Macdonald concluded to his horror, that any trigger-happy hooligan, no matter what his experience, training or emotional stability, could take out a license to hunt animals. If he hit a human, that was just the breaks of the game.

So Macdonald persuaded his employers to cooperate in his scheme. He found a blind lawyer with a guide dog and took him to a downtown Seattle hardware store to buy a hunting license. The store not only sold the blind lawyer a hunting license, but also was glad to sell him a supply of ammunition and a 12-gauge shotgun. When Macdonald's disk jockeys were turned loose with this intelligence, abashed state officials tightened up the hunting license regulations and an eye check was made mandatory.

These were, as I've indicated, days of wine and roses. I would foregather with the flacks at such places as the old Emel Hotel (now the Kennedy) bar, the Olympic Grill, and more often at what might be called the old New Grove, then operated by Les Brainerd and since run by several less successful entrepreneurs. A bartender named Jimmy Spellman poured freehand, and to favored regulars he might hold the bottle high and long enough until, in the words of Jimmy Breslin, "you got a drink that would make a mule walk backward." It is useless to estimate how many livers were permanently damaged in these places, especially the old New Grove, but for years the latter was a hangout for prominent jocks, beat reporters, sportswriters, and, of course, our lovable geniuses, the press agents.

Into these precincts entered a smooth-faced, handsome bear of a kid who was the assistant PR for a local television station. He usually came with his boss, a redoubtable fellow named Mel Anderson, and the kid dutifully kept up his end of the wisecracking and three-Scotch revelry. The kid and I became good friends in subsequent years, although he had, much earlier, resigned from these long scrimmages which began with some regularity at five-thirty each afternoon. "I decided that the track was not for me," he told me some years later. "Something had to give—my job, my career, my marriage—if I stayed with that crew. So I included myself out." It proved to be a wise choice. Eric Bremner is now vice-president of KING Broadcasting's chain of television and radio stations in Washington, Oregon and Idaho.

The press agent—a good one, that is—comes to terms early with the fact that his work usually goes unrecognized, except among a small group of his peers, or among reporters used to the machinations of his dark art. If the press agent's venture is a success, if it gets the kind of coverage he was hired to provide, the credit usually goes to the reporter or columnist working under a byline, or to a radio or television person who puts his stuff on the air. In some twenty-six years of scratching together column ideas, of feeding a column with human interest features, I came to fear those inevitable, desperate days. A toothache, a hangover, a personal problem, or just a case of the blahs, calls up a huge empty space in a panic-stricken mind's eye. That is when the true pros of the PR racket are invaluable, people like Jack Macdonald, Guy Williams, Bill Sears, the late Bob Woolson, Sharon Friel, Bill Marsh, Ken Fleming, Jim Faber—and so many others who scratched up material to bail me out.

Thus it is the mark of a press agent—again, the good one—that he frequently comes up with ideas or news notes that cannot possibly help his client. I used to keep a private "don't use" list of people who called only when they had something to sell. A wise press agent is one who keeps on sending stuff even when it doesn't concern his client. One distinct hazard of the press agent's trade is that his client soon comes to believe that seeing his name in print is the way life ought to be, that his overlooked genius in the commercial scheme of things is at last being given the public recognition it deserves. The human ego is a marvel to behold.

When he has been at it long enough, the press agent is aware that the better he does his job the more likely he is to work himself out of it. It is also true that when a recession cuts profits, clients tend to trim the one person they need most—the guy who can keep the company's light from being hidden behind the nearest bushel. But a good press agent, fortunately, has the survival instinct of a nocturnal bat.

One of the best press agents I know is a jovial, portly

bohunk named Bill Dugovich. His demeanor, which is in-genuous, forthright and informal, does not square with some of the clients he has served. He once got national publicity for Tacoma's water system, of all things, and in his time he has hustled publicity for hotels, restaurants, resorts, or just for people he happened to like.

For several years, Bill Dugovich worked on behalf of what was once known as Western International Hotels. This company, now renamed Westin Hotels, enjoyed considerable public esteem largely because its president, the estimable Eddie Carlson, was a doer of civic good works. Regrettably for Western International Hotels, Carlson left to head up United Airlines. But Dugovich remained to work wonders for this growing hotel chain. He did it by getting to know a lot of or-dinary people in the company, by pounding out his own stories, feeding trade publications, business magazines and the general press with the kind of stuff that reflects credit on an organization. To my personal knowledge, he devised and sold a number of important (and friendly) feature stories on company executives.

Then one day it was decided that some corporate deity in the sky could handle such mere details. Some middle man-agement yahoo called Bill Dugovich in and fired him. They gave him no particular reason, but there were vague mumblings afterward that Western International Hotels did not think he quite matched the fashion of their "corporate image." So Bill Dugovich, without complaining to anyone, packed up his ideas and goodwill and went elsewhere. Which is why stories about Westin Hotels rarely appear anywhere except in routine business accounts of the corporation.

The more or less anonymous role of the flack makes it understandable why people believe that such things as the

World's Fair and the Kingdome just happened. It is unlikely that many among the millions who attend events in the Kingdome have even heard of Bill Sears and Mel Anderson. But together, this pair (along with a couple of sharp ad guys, Jerry Hoeck and Jack Ehrig) helped convince voters that the Kingdome bond issue might be a good thing. Sears and Anderson both worked on two other such bond issues, which failed, but they finally won out in 1968—a Herculean job when you consider that the money measure needed 60 percent approval by the voters.

The anonymity of the press agent is best exemplified by Mel Anderson, the king of them all, who never allowed his name or his picture to be connected with any of his ventures. Not if he could help it. But his exploits over the years insured that Anderson himself would be better remembered than his clients; such was the boldness of his imagination and the magnetism of his personality. And Anderson, more than most of his kind, scorned such lofty titles as "media consultant," and preferred to be known for what he is, "the last of the real press agents—nothing more, nothing less."

Because of his standing in the trade, so to speak, he frequently is called in to pump up some "establishment" promotion, such as Seafair or the World's Fair. He does not impress easily. On one occasion a Seattle bank, anxious to get tied into promoting a professional tennis exhibition, hired Anderson "to create a little fanfare," as they put it. One who was at the first meeting describes the picture of Anderson, silently chewing on his ever present cigar, as a dozen bankers talked up their tennis promotion. During the entire meeting, Anderson said only a few words, then got up and left. Two weeks passed. No publicity. Not a word in the papers or a breath of tennis on the air. "Who is this guy Anderson?" one of the bankers complained. "If he's such a hot-shot, where's the publicity? We can do better calling on the papers ourselves."

A few more days passed. Then, as though someone had turned on a spigot, a veritable deluge of stories began to appear in the region's papers. Disc jockeys talked up the tournament on the air. The newspaper stories appeared not only on the sports pages, but turned up in what was then known as the society page as well. "What happened is that Mel bailed them all out of a bad promotion," one friend told me later. "I don't know if Mel ever saw the bankers again, or if they even asked how he did it. Maybe they just thought they had it coming."

"I'll tell you how he did it," says Bill Sears, "he did it because he was Mel Anderson. He probably prowled the halls, telling jokes about tennis, pretending he didn't care much about it. He probably didn't. But without anyone quite knowing it, he passed on tips and angles and wisecracks, and like I say, he was Mel Anderson. He never gave anyone a bum steer and he had built up such a fund of good feeling that anything Mel did was irresistible."

Mel Anderson belongs in the company of hucksterism's great names—he is the stuff of Wilson Mizener, Bob Hannegan, P.T. Barnum and Jack Hurley. The latter enjoyed an advantage over most press agents. What he sold he owned, meaning that his product was boxers, whom Hurley manipulated and ruled with an iron hand. So his clients, unlike many who hire press agents, were not squeamish or impatient; they were instructed to shut up, do what they were told, and to forget what they read about themselves in the papers.

Anderson's creative imagination functions within a firm,

self-imposed structure of ethics; his integrity and character would pass him unscathed through a Lutheran loyalty hearing. His talent is composed of a fertile imagination, a wit that is 3.2 percent sharper than mustard, and an ability to speak with detached amusement about what he is up to. All that, plus an uncanny ability to convince you that his clients are worthy, if not saintly.

During the 1950s he did much to elevate KING television and radio into city institutions; the station's on-air personalities had a way of appearing in news stories that irritated KING's less favored rivals. A chat with Anderson, laced with humor, could leave you with the impression that Mrs. Dorothy Bullitt, the station's owner, combined only the best qualities of Eleanor Roosevelt, Helen Hayes and Madame Curie; that the station manager, Otto Brandt, would be heading up the Ford Foundation were it not for his devotion to further elevating KING's quality air time; that KING's on-air people like Chuck Herring, Casey Gregorson, Al Cumings and "Sheriff Tex" lived only to enlighten and amuse our city. News and feature writers flock as lemmings around Mel Anderson, and to say he "maneuvers" or "uses" the press connotes the same redundancy as pulling a nymphomaniac into bed.

Thus he can and did take a "nothing event" like the King County Fair at Enumclaw and turn it into one of the region's most successful agricultural shows. Fair goers began to hear of Henrietta, a prize goose, that was chosen Critter Queen of the fair. He turned the cleanup crew into the Solid Waste Management Drill Team and Marching Band. In one of his rare interviews, Anderson told the *Seattle Times'* Don Duncan that one of his toughest jobs was "to convince the owner of a prize horse that the little girl who had just baked a plate of cookies was just as important as he was." He may have failed in that, but the fair succeeded.

In his time, Mel Anderson has promoted Gene Autry, Liberace, Lawrence Welk, the Harlem Globetrotters and two different ice shows in alternate months. "The idea is to get yourself out of the way," he told Duncan, "because nobody pays a nickel at the box office to watch a press agent."

I mentioned earlier that press agents—at least the old-style, Barnumesque types—are on the endangered species list. This is depressingly true. The inimitable Guy Williams is now seventy-seven and semi-retired; Bob Ward and Mel Anderson are in their mid-sixties. Others, like Jack Gordon and Jim Faber, have more or less turned the game back to the boys.

Finally, let us not forget Bill Speidel. It was Speidel who first publicized and sold the idea of preserving Seattle's rundown skid road and turning it into chic Pioneer Square. Speidel lives in semi-retirement, partly supported by one of his earlier and still popular schemes—the notion that thousands of people will pay to take (as they do) underground tours of Pioneer Square. "It may be that Bill Speidel is better than all of us," mused one press agent not long ago. "Who else could support himself by selling a hole in the ground?"

5

The Voice of Summer

"*Freddy Muller digs in that back foot, taps the plate lightly with his bat, now he cocks it high off his shoulder—he's got power, hits the fast ball very well . . . outfield is shaded slightly to the left. . . . Shellenback takes his sign, goes into his windup—once around, twice around—here it is. Shelly caught the outside corner of the plate with a fast ball. Strike one. Muller didn't like that call. Turns and says something to the umpire. . . . Now he's ready again. . . . Shellenback goes into his delivery—it's a long, high fly, going for the left field fence, going . . . going . . . going . . . and it's OVER! Oh, baby, did he ever hit that one!*"

That voice.

It came through the speaker of our old radio, when Mr. Atwater and Mr. Kent were very big in the business of making radios. The voice of Leo Lassen riveted your attention, the sharp tones now confidential, now high pitched, an almost staccato-like delivery, a voice that could set nerves on edge, but a voice that imparted a sense of urgency, drama and importance to a game being played miles away. I would sit up each night, hanging on Leo Lassen's every word, and those heroes of Seattle he talked about—Freddy Muller, Mel Almada, Fritz Knothe, Charley Borriani, Jerry Donovan, Johnny Bassler—they were heroes of a city kid stuck out in the country.

I hated my dad's farm. My father, who probably never knew what a work ethic was, who never consulted the dictums of Calvin and Luther, was a bear for work. And on a farm, it was nothing but work. He had bought this farm, out near Carnation (known as Tolt then) and he tried to stave off the Great Depression by being his own man on his own land. I was sadly deficient in my father's eyes. He was a man of varied abilities, a carpenter, a blacksmith, a mover of houses, a farmer who believed that a farm should be a proud place—a place where you lived independently of outside needs. To this end, I could be trusted with gathering the eggs, milking a cow, bringing in wood, or doing any of the "chores" that required no long attention span. But my heart wasn't in it. I was a city kid, raised on pavement, nurtured on playgrounds and sand lots, roller hockey on tennis courts, and I got bored with stringing peas, forking hay; my father despaired that I would amount to much. He was probably right.

In performing such tedious tasks as harrowing, or extensive hoeing, my fantasies constantly diverted me into minor disasters. Plants, not the weeds, would get hoed; the horses, sensing a loose rein, would wander. "Stop daydreaming!" my father would command, to no avail. I was a "partner" to Tom Mix, I made up new lyrics to old songs; trying to imitate Leo Lassen's shrill voice, I concocted entire baseball games, using memorized lineups of the old Seattle Indians, the San Francisco Seals and the Los Angeles Angels. My father feared that I would grow up to become, as he put it, "an atha-letic bum." He could not understand my fixation for Leo Lassen and the gibberish (to him) that Leo talked in those evening hours, every week, every month, every summer. "That fella sure talks fast," was the only grudging tribute I ever heard him utter about Leo Lassen.

That voice.

It was a voice that I and hundreds of thousands would be fixed on for nearly thirty years. I didn't know it then, but that voice would have an effect on my life, and I would get to know the man who owned it. I really did hate the farm, and Leo's voice, a staccato siren song, kept drawing me back to the city, making me want to be where I could hear streetcars again, be around bats and balls and movies every Friday night, with Sunday doubleheaders in the sunshine. Someday, I vowed, I would play for the Seattle Indians and Leo Lassen would be talking about me. Dreams of glory. But the farm was very real then. As a "city kid" I wasn't much accepted by my peers. Because I only milked two or three cows, I was looked down upon by kids who milked eighteen or twenty.

The railroad tracks passed by our farm and also behind the school about a mile away. I got so good at walking a single rail that I could do the entire mile without losing balance. An old wooden railroad bridge once spanned the Tolt River and the bridge had barrels spaced beside the tracks so water would be available in case of fire. I learned to smoke with an old cigarette brand called "One-11's" which I used to stash in a water barrel before I got home from school. They cost eleven cents. My father's farm is now part of the famous Remlinger

Farm, headquarters for the Remlinger U-Pick berry empire. The Remlingers built a beautiful brick home up on the hill above the stream where I once caught sluggish "dog salmon" by the tail. Their new home was built around the old Watson farmhouse, keeping some of the framework, and when I visit there, occasionally, I still can see what was once my bedroom window.

I'd lie awake in that bedroom reading *Tom Sawyer* and *Huckleberry Finn*, tons of Zane Grey, great stacks of pulp westerns, and one of my favorites was a zippy old magazine called *Captain Billy's Whiz Bang*. They didn't have any sex education in Carnation grade school, but who needed that when your older brother left *Captain Billy's Whiz Bang* lying around? All that reading, of course, was secondary and came after Leo Lassen's sign-off from another broadcast.

"That evens the series at two games apiece. Once again, for those who tuned in late, the score was San Francisco 5, Seattle 2. The line score: San Francisco, five runs, nine hits and no errors . . . Seattle, three runs, seven hits and one error. The winning pitcher was Win Ballou, the loser Dutch Reuther. Again, it was an exciting evening of baseball. I enjoyed bringing you this play-by-play account, but come to the ball park when you can. Nothing beats the real thing. Uh . . . this is Leo Lassen saying good night once again. It was a grand evening of baseball. I hope you enjoyed it."

Enjoyed it? We lived it. God, how I wished to be there for the "real thing." But I was stuck on that farm in the bottom of the Great Depression. My father couldn't sell anything he grew. One year it was peas. We must have raised enough peas that summer to feed an emerging African nation. I had to hoe them and I had to string them and I had to pick them. We all did. And do you know how many peas we sold? Not one goddamned pea. So the end of all this labor was that we loaded these boxes of peas on a truck and my father, a fine and generous man, drove them into Seattle and went door to door, visiting his old neighbors and friends, giving these peas away to the people who now needed any food they could get.

When he lost the farm to the bank, we had to move back to the city and go on welfare. The Depression killed my old man, as much as anything else did. He had pride. He took pride in hard work, in running a self-sufficient farm, where we made our own butter, slaughtered our own pigs, cured our own hams, raised chickens and ducks, stored potatoes in the root cellar to feed the pigs and ran the primitive farm machinery out of my dad's own blacksmith shop. He was an all-purpose man, my dad, but the Depression killed him. When he lost the farm to the bank and we moved back to Seattle, where he had to stand in line at the commissary on California Ave., it broke this wonderful, tough, hard-working man. The spirit went out of him, the way it did with so many other fine men like him, men crushed by distant forces of economics that they couldn't understand.

Back in the city you did what you could. My dad tried selling fish out of a truck he paneled and packed with ice. He got an odd job now and then, but nothing lasted. Mostly he had to stand in the commissary line. For a while I hustled the *Times,* the *P–I* and the *Star* at Spokane St. and Marginal Way, under the old streetcar trestle, then I latched onto a choice corner at the intersection of Admiral Way and California Ave. One afternoon I was late getting to my corner and my dad was there, a broad, heavyset man, wearing his "police" suspenders, and looking slightly embarrassed as I arrived.

"I was just passing by, son," he said. "I thought I'd

unbundle the papers and maybe sell a few before you got here. Any time you need help, let me know. I can come here early and cover for you." He was lying, and I knew it, and he knew I knew it. He wasn't just "passing by." He had these endless discouraging days of time on his hands; no job, no money, no hope. In our household I was the only one making any cash, however pitiful it was, and he felt it was his duty as a father to help me. So we carried on the charade, and he went away from there, walking down the street, legs slightly bowed, limping a bit because of an accident he'd had when he was forced to jump off a runaway truck. It was the first time in my life I ever cried for anyone except myself.

"Now he stretches, now he sets. Barrett isn't very fast, but he's got that curve ball. Boy, has he got a curve ball! DiMaggio cocks the bat. The delivery! Strike two, and he cracked off a curve ball down around the knees! Now Barrett takes his stretch again. Kicks the leg and pumps to the plate. . . . Foul tip, back at the catcher. Oh, baby, if you've never been hit by a foul tip, you don't know what you've missed!"

The voice.

Only the names were new, the voice endured.

It floated out of open doors in every neighborhood on warm summer nights, sometimes low and confidential, often high and piercing, occasionally reaching a crescendo of excitement. "It's a line drive—bing, bing!—there it is!"

In West Seattle I was raised with a large Irish Catholic family, the Nokes. There was "Pa" Nokes and "Ma" Nokes and Ed and Joe and Tom and Lorraine and Gene and Pat and Katy and Jerry and Mary and Bob and they were wonderful. When I wasn't home I was at the Nokes' house, where the place erupted in frequent small riots of laughter, because all of them were blessed with a gorgeous sense of humor, a gift for mimicry, and a theatrical appreciation of the absurd. If you bumped your head, Ma Nokes rubbed butter on it, if she had any butter, but I could never figure out why. Joe could do superb imitations of FDR holding a "fireside chat" ("Mah friends, when Ah took office in thutty-three, the banks were closed!") and Pat could "do" Leo Lassen quite well. Everybody imitated Leo's voice. We wore our hair long not as social protest, but because barbers cost money. We never heard of marijuana, but "snipe-hunting" was much in style; that, or you rolled your own Bull Durham. In those days there was no such thing as "motivational analysis" tests for getting a job. The right man for the job was the guy who got there first and often lied most convincingly about his qualifications. Air pollution was no problem because the mills weren't fired up—we'd see smoke coming out of the Bethlehem Steel plant at the bottom of Admiral Way and think, "Hey, maybe we've found the corner." That meant the "corner" which prosperity was always supposed to be around, but never was.

West Seattle is more a city of its own than a Seattle neighborhood—so big it has neighborhoods of its own. Before buses and better streets, it was a good hour's ride into the city from West Seattle, at least on the streetcar. To give you an idea, if you've never been there: West Seattle has nine miles of waterfront, 410 acres of parks, including Schmitz Park, a virgin forest, and is generally believed to be 15.7 square miles in size. West Seattle is bigger than Bellevue and the principality of Monaco combined, and it probably attracts a better class of people.

West Seattle has better views than Magnolia, more trees

than Lake Washington Boulevard and Volunteer Park combined, more millionaires than Broadmoor. In it reside enough
Boeing super-technicians to build its own missile system. For
better or worse, West Seattle is where the whole city got
started. The schooner *Exact* landed where we built beach fires
as kids. That is to say, the *Exact* came in loaded with mothers,
fathers, dogs and several barrels of whiskey near Alki Point
and there is a marker to prove it. They were digging clams on
Alki beach before the first tree was felled on Queen Anne
Hill.

Tell somebody you live in Laurelhurst, Beacon Hill, Ballard
or Wallingford and they usually get the idea. Tell them, "I
live in West Seattle," and they usually ask, "What part?" The
answer is rarely precise. In West Seattle you live "down on
Beach Drive," or "up on 35th," or "near the junction." The
"junction," which is actually the intersection of Alaska St.
and California Ave., is a good mile away from another well-
known reference point, the corner of California Ave. and
Admiral Way. That makes you a "north West Seattleite,"
which is what I was.

California Ave. is the longest street in Seattle and, in many
ways, the city's lengthiest abomination. The exception is
Aurora, which isn't a street, really, but a death trap of heavy
traffic, neon lights, fast food places, used car lots and hot
pillow joints. West Seattle is a mix of individual districts, poor
next to rich, like new beans and leftover pasta in a good
minestrone. The West Seattle I knew as a kid was all white,
baby, and don't you forget it. You didn't find any Japanese or
blacks or Filipinos in those days, and it wasn't until I moved
away from there that I really got the hang of nature's color
chart.

By the mid-1930s, my life was set. I would be a professional baseball player. That voice again. All through the Depression, it was part of our young existence, and Leo's dramatized portrayals of baseball games seemed to drench the city in summer, and for many of us, so young then, he fueled our dreams, even set our goals and ambitions. "Hang onto those rocking chairs!"—that was a Leo gambit we parroted in any unusual situation.

"Barrett pitches . . . it's a long, high fly going deep to left center field wall. . . . Lawrence is going back, back, back—he caught it, he caught it! Oh, baby, did he ever come up with one! Old 'High Pockets' Bill Lawrence was off at the crack of the bat, those long strides eating up ground, and he pulled it in high off the left center field fence. Umm, baby what a catch!"

In Red Colbert's hamburger shack across from Hiawatha Playfield we listened to that voice which described the deeds of demi-gods; minor league demi-gods, to be sure, but heroes who made gobs of money when everyone else was out of work. It was only later that Bill Lawrence told me that in those glory years he had to fight and argue to get $400 a month—the best center fielder in the league. Many years after, "Dutch" Reuther, who managed the old Indians of 1936, told me how the owner, Bill Klepper, gave him all the gate receipts to hide from the sheriff, due at the ball park to collect back admissions taxes. "I had all those damned dollar bills stuffed down in my baseball pants when I was coaching third base," Dutch recalled. "And if I'd a had a shortstop that year I'd a won the pennant by fifteen games."

But in those early years of our adolescent yearnings for recognition, Leo Lassen's voice was a call that beckoned—wealth and fame, the glory and the dream. It was settled then.

I would be a ball player. Every morning, every afternoon, we played baseball and more baseball. When we weren't playing it, we hitchhiked down to old Civic Field, where Memorial Stadium stands now, so we could imitate the batting style and posturings of our heroes. Civic Field was a magnificent old sieve-like place, where you could sneak in by a dozen routes. To pay your way into a game (economically unfeasible anyway) would be a loss of face. So we saw them all come through on their way to the "big leagues"—Joe and Dominic DiMaggio, Dolf Camilli, Earle Brucker, Alan Strange, Ted Williams, dozens of others.

I got out of West Seattle High School then—my grades in shambles—before the principal, Mr. Reed Fulton, got around to suggesting my departure first. In the fall I was an equipment rat for the old West Seattle Yellowjackets football team, one of whose assistant coaches was a kindly guy named "Pop" Reed, who held a singular attraction in my eyes. He coached baseball at Franklin High School. Franklin High School won games, and they had a dizzying array of prep stars then, including a thin-lipped, stone-faced kid named Fred Hutchinson.

With Pop Reed's help, I boarded out in a house on Beacon Hill. It was only the second of many neighborhoods I have lived in, but Beacon Hill held no special attraction at the time, except that it was in the Franklin High School district. The main thing I remember about Beacon Hill was the wearying long climb it took from Rainier Ave. to the top of McClellan St. after baseball practice. Later my mom moved into Rainier Valley, so I could live with her again and stay in the school district. She was a wonderful woman, my mom. She didn't know anything about baseball but she knew the pain kids suffered in growing up; knowing nothing about baseball, she nevertheless came dutifully to all the games I played.

Jesus, we were good! In the next two years we scarcely lost a game and in the final year we were undefeated. Hutch and Bud Castro would regularly spin out two and three-hitters, and Hutch usually drove in a few runs himself. We had a big, awkward kid named Dewey Soriano, who not only played first base but fired a mean fast ball that used to cause bone bruises on my catching hand. There was Ray Tran, Cy Stephens, Ralph Yorio, Dick Wake, Carl Wienker, Ernie Endress, Bud Castro and too many others to list. Pop Reed, because of our celebrity, could get us in free at old Civic Field to watch the Indians, where Dewey, and his brother Rupe, sold peanuts to help out the family. In the final year, among those who started, virtually all of us signed professional contracts after graduation. Major league scouts were hanging around in clusters—Hutch was the big attraction. We beat everybody in sight—regular opponents (we once beat Broadway High, 38–4), semi-pros, the Washington frosh; we beat them all. Pop Reed treated us as royalty, sometimes taking two or three of us to the old Richelieu Cafe at Seventh and Union, where we ate huge T-bone steaks that cost the obscene price of a dollar. Because he liked me, Pop tried to get the scouts interested, even pushing my case to Ernie Johnson, of the Boston Red Sox. Johnson's reply was ominous. "I know you think he's a good kid," he told Reed, "but I have to ask this—doesn't he *ever* get a base hit?"

The year after I left school they built Sicks' Stadium, which was what you might call sneak-in proof. Civic Field's rattly tin fence, topped by barbed wire, with leaky entries that made it easy to climb over or wriggle through, was a thing of the past. Now we had to pay. But what we got was a beautiful, symmetrical, clean park, with manicured grass and pebble-free dirt around the bases. I got odd jobs by then, and I would buy a ticket to the bleachers where Hutch, only eighteen years old, stood the whole Pacific Coast League on its ear, winning twenty-five games in his first season and scoring his nineteenth victory on his nineteenth birthday. I sat out with the roped-in crowd in center field for that one. After Rainier games we sometimes met our buddy, Hutch, now known reverently throughout the city as The Iceman. With Hutch we drank root beer at the Triple-X Barrel where, only a year before, we had drunk root beer in triumph at Franklin High.

Thus began the glory years of the new Seattle Rainiers, who would shatter all attendance records in minor league baseball; the sale of Hutch to Detroit brought a plethora of talent, including the incomparable Jo-Jo White, and pennants duly came in 1939, 1940 and 1941. The old Seattle Indians, chronic losers, gave way to these spiffy, classy champions and the city went wild over them. The summers passed.

"White leads off first, dancing, dancing, ready to break. He's driving the pitcher crazy. . . . Strange is up there now, hitting second . . . umm, baby, hear that crowd yell. Oh, you should be here tonight! Mount Rainier is out beyond the right field fence, looming up like a great . . . big . . . ice cream cone. There he goes! Strange lashes a hard-hit line drive through the vacant hole at second, and here's White . . . rounding second, going to third . . . lookit him run! Oh, baby, are those Rainiers ever hot!"

How I got in four years of college ball without getting caught for cheating is a minor mystery. I played for the university in the afternoon and at semi-pro parks at night, where I picked up $5.00 or $7.50 a game. Tubby Graves, the Washington coach, knew all about this chicanery, but he didn't say anything, because Tubby Graves knew that $15.00 a month on a National Youth Administration job didn't go far, even in those days. I played for a no-nonsense guy named Babe Barberis, who put together exciting, well-disciplined bush-league teams, and we roamed over western Washington, playing Bremerton, Shelton, Bellingham, Renton and Tacoma. That illegal dough helped me through school.

What did you do in baseball, daddy? Well, kiddies, I once hit against Satchell Paige. I once faced the great black legend who had beaten such teams as the New York Yankees, the Cleveland Indians and the St. Louis Cardinals; who took the measure of great white pitchers like Bob Feller and Dizzy Dean, whose blinding fast ball mowed down all-star casts of the greatest players in major league history. Satch, barred from white baseball because of his color, came to town on tour with the awesome Kansas City Monarchs. I don't remember the score of that game, but I remember numb, shaking knees as I stepped in against this man who could make a baseball look the size of an aspirin tablet. I hit one off him, too. Not a base hit. Not much of anything. Satch just reared up, flailing his long arms, and instead of the dreaded blazer, he threw a soft, looping curve, which I hit to second base for a ground-out. I got his autograph after the game.

The Rainiers called me in the summer of 1942. They got a catcher hurt and would I consider signing a contract? I was delirious. Torchy Torrance, long a dynamic figure in Seattle's civic affairs, was then a vice-president of the Rainiers. He called me into a back room beyond the showers in the main clubhouse. "We'd like to take you on the next road trip with us," he said. "You'll be gone three weeks. Can you make it?"

A rookie can usually make it when they lay out an invitation like that. "We'll give you $250 a month," he said. "Sign here." I went out of there thinking, "This man's crazy! He's giving me a fortune to play ball."

They released me at the end of the road trip when their injured catcher returned to action. They promised to bring me back for spring training in 1943. By now, of course, that overseas unpleasantness had escalated into a full-scale war. Many of the real professionals were gone from baseball, taken into the service, but even with this chance, I was on shaky ground. It came to an end after spring training in 1943, when, after two weeks on the road in San Diego and Sacramento, the Rainiers opened at Sicks' Stadium. Imbedded deep in the P-I archives is a story of that game, written by Leo Lassen, who doubled as baseball's official "voice" in Seattle by writing up the games. The story tells how the Rainiers, before this opening day crowd, faltered and failed. It told how San Francisco hit well with men on bases, how a pitcher named Bill Harrell throttled us, and how we committed several miscues that led to this 9–1 debacle. I now refer you to a poignant paragraph that graphically described how Seattle scored its only run:

"Demoran singled to open Seattle's half of that inning (the third). Bill Katz nearly tore the glove off Keystoner Del Young with another one-baser. Emmett Watson (that's me, folks) went in to run for Demoran at second base." To this day, I don't know why Bill Skiff, our manager, sent me in to run, but I heard his voice above the roar of the crowd: "Watson, get in there for Demoran." I was stunned. So, for that matter, was the entire Rainier bench, all of them fully aware that I could scarcely outrun the average kitchen table. "Emmy, get out there!" somebody yelled, breaking my trance. I trotted out to second and replaced Demoran. The score at that time was only 2–0 against us. Passing me on the basepath, Demoran growled, "Don't get picked off, Emmy." Picked off? I may have been dumb, but I wasn't about to get picked off in front of all those hometown fans.

Lassen's account continues: "Lynn King whiffed. But Bill Lawrence blasted a single to right and Watson was nearly picked off third base on the relay from Metokovich to catcher Bruce Ogrodowski to third-sacker Charley Peterson."

There it is, the bald truth. Rounding third base, trying to score on Bill Lawrence's single, I fell down. Nothing more. Nothing less. No alibis. I just fell down. Caught between third and home, I scrambled back to third like a panicked seal making for shore with a killer whale in pursuit. I barely beat the relay pickoff throw to third. "There is one out," I said to myself. "If we don't score this run, I am the laughing stock of opening day." Lassen's story concluded:

"Bill Matheson poled a tremendous fly which Frenchy Uhalt gathered in, and Watson scored after the catch. But Dick Gyselman grounded out and the threat was over."

That is not all that was over. The next day Mr. Skiff took me aside. "It is time to make some changes," he said. "I mean, it is time for you to leave. You are a nice kid, but you have—ah, too many handicaps." Skiffy was a kind and diplomatic man. By using the term "handicaps" he hoped I would assume he meant my bad hearing. That would let me down easy, but it didn't. That was the most memorable game I ever played. What did you do in the Coast League, daddy? Well, I got a pop fly single as a pinch-hitter and grounded out another time. Lifetime batting average, preserved forever in the record book: .500. On that disastrous day of the 1943 season opener, they awarded prizes for "firsts"—first hit, first walk, first run scored, etc. For scoring that first run I got an $18.75 war bond. Joe Demoran was outraged.

"That is *my* war bond," he insisted. "I got the hit, I got to second. If Skiffy hadn't put you in, I would have scored that run. You even fell down before you scored, Emmy. Gimme my war bond." "Go to hell, Joe," I said. "I scored the run, I get the bond. Besides, I'm out of work and I need the money."

What did you do in the war, daddy? I did what almost everybody else did, those who were 4-F in the draft, or had dependents. There were ration books and "meat points" and "A" cards and "B" cards and "C" cards for gas. I worked at Todd Shipyard for a dollar an hour, a princely wage, playing bush ball at night and on weekends for ten bucks a game. I got a job on the old *Seattle Star*, covering the team I once played for, the Rainiers, and it was evident that Bill Skiff, still the manager, didn't think any more of my writing than he did of my base-running. I worked for the *Star*, then the *Times*, then the *P–I*, doing columns, writing features, and describing endless hundreds of baseball games. Leo Lassen's voice still was a big part of my life.

"Now he's ready, now the delivery . . . ground ball to the shortstop's right . . . over to second, over to first—it's a double playyy! Here comes O'Doul out of the dugout. Lefty didn't like that call at first. He's arguing with the first-base umpire, Jack Powell. The umpire walks away, O'Doul follows him. Baby, is he hot! Oh, for the life of an umpire!"

Now I listened to Leo Lassen in a different way. Because I would be late to some games—or would have to stay in the office to transcribe games that were played on the road—I began to appreciate Lassen's true worth. He was above all, a reporter, and he had a good reporter's passion for accuracy. One could jot down his accounts of the game and, because he didn't miss a thing, you could turn to a typewriter and write your own graphic version of the game, based on descriptive facts, the facts voiced and recorded by Leo.

On some nights after games Leo and I would go out and drink together. He was slow to accept me at first. It took several of these sessions to ease my self-consciousness about being with Leo—the remembrance that he was, to me, the man whose voice did much to shape the entertainment values of Seattle for so many years. His voice still sounded the way it did when I huddled close to the old Atwater-Kent radio and dreamed the dreams of a farm kid, yearning for the city.

Leo didn't drink often, but when he did it was a plunge for distance. Sometimes we stayed out until four and five in the morning. He talked baseball, only baseball—that was his life and his consuming passion. As the Scotch flowed, his voice would raise, and its laser-like penetration shook up patrons several tables away. Leo had one slightly withered arm, the result of a childhood fall. As I came to know him better, the realization came that Leo was—well, somehow "different." It was nothing I could define then, until I heard the colorful old ticket broker, Frank Hixon, tell him, "Lassen, why don't you go out with a woman sometime—just as a decoy?" But that didn't matter, although it may have explained his obsession with talking about a game played by boys and men.

I even came to the conclusion that Leo was strangely miscast as a sports announcer. His nasal voice drove some people up walls, but more important, it seemed to me, his sensitivity and intellect would preclude his need for a game that kids could play. He read the classics—Dickens was his favorite, "because he was a great reporter"—and he could compose and play classical music on the piano. I was surprised to learn that he was once managing editor of the *Star*—in those days when the *Star* was a lively, crusading paper—and he exploded many front-page stories with his imaginative news judgment. But he got fired from that when the Scripps people, troglodytes of the cash register, whose regard for the First Amendment was about equal to their devotion to a traffic ordinance, chopped him off because his salary was too high—fifty dollars a week.

One night as we sat up late drinking, I asked him a question. "Remember that base hit I got in San Diego back in 1943?" I asked. "Why shouldn't I, it was the only hit you got," he said. I said, "Well, look, that game was played in San Diego and you were recreating that broadcast off the teletype up here. It was a pop fly that fell in, but since I was a hometown kid, why didn't you make it into a line drive?" "Because I'm a reporter, you silly son of a bitch, and don't ever forget that," he laughed. "I may not be fancy, but I'm fast and accurate."

It was the 1950s, a wonderful time to be in Seattle. The Rainiers won the pennant in 1955. Two of my old teammates, Hutch and Dewey Soriano, took over the Rainiers. Hutch had gone farther and stayed longer than any Seattle sports figure in the city's history. At Dewey's behest, he quit the Detroit Tigers, where he was one of baseball's youngest managers, and returned to Seattle. Together, Dewey and Hutch tore the team apart, making sixty-three separate player deals that season, and Seattle would win its pennant. None of us quite realized that baseball, as a big-time Seattle sport, had peaked for the last time.

Other things were happening. Boeing rolled out the first

707 and with it came a revolution in air travel. The Supreme Court came down like a ton of bricks with its school integration decision of 1954. Grace Kelly married her Graustarkian prince, and Russia sent up a contraption to the atmosphere that rained down the message, "beep . . . beep . . . beep" on the nation's radios. James Hagerty, the White House press secretary, and other members of the Eisenhower administration, tried to play down the significance of Sputnik I. But my old friend Bob Ward called the next morning and said, "Do you realize what that means? It means those bastards can turn loose a shot that will land right on the I-key of Hagerty's typewriter."

The Hungarian Freedom Fighters rose and revolted, but eight Soviet divisions, seven of them armored, went in and crushed the uprising. Some thirty thousand Hungarians were killed and perhaps twice as many banished to Siberia. A strange creature named Orval Faubus, whose like we would see again and again as the full impact of the Court's school decision was felt, barred black children from entering white schools in Arkansas. Eisenhower, the golf-playing, pacifying president, refused to do what people wanted him to do—go to Little Rock and lead a black kid into the schoolroom, a symbolic and inspiring gesture, a message that here was a president who wanted the law of the land upheld. And Mort Sahl, an emerging satiric comedian with a wolfish grin and a rolled-up newspaper, got a big laugh when he said, "That's a hard decision for Eisenhower to make. After all, when you take a child by the hand, do you use the interlocking or the overlapping grip?" Dr. Jonas Salk developed the vaccine that would rid the world of polio and a bearded guerrilla, wearing fatigues and combat boots, came out of the hills in Cuba to overthrow Batista.

Maybe it was the times, the far places, the romance, or the age, but just being around baseball wasn't fun any more. Not that I could ever hope to cover these stories, but I did stumble into an exclusive interview with Ernest Hemingway. For the first time, Hemingway spoke out on the subject of Cuba, where he lived and wrote, and my copyrighted stories went around the world. It was blind luck and I wrote it badly, but it was much headier stuff than snapping jock straps and fighting for tidbits of sports news that nobody seemed to care about. Earlier, I had gone in to see Ed Stone, the *P-I*'s managing editor, and said I had to get off the baseball beat. It was a decision long coming. I was tired of baseball. I had traveled to dozens of cities and all I had collected was a hazy recollection of airports, hotel lobbies and half-warm hot dogs in press boxes. Stone seemed to understand.

"Ummm, baby, you should see the moon tonight from Sicks' Stadium, out there like a great ball of fire . . . what a beautiful night for baseball in Seattle. The windup. Here's the pitch . . . a high pop fly, a MILE in the air . . . the inning is over, and for the Rainiers it's—"

Suddenly, Leo was gone from the air. For whatever reason, a salary squabble, a fight with the station, no matter; his broadcasting career was over. He had left once before, absent during the single season of 1957, but that time nobody doubted that Leo would return. Indeed, he did return, because Emil Sick, the splendid owner of the Rainiers, wanted him back, so Leo resumed broadcasting on another station. But this time, three years later, it was for good, and for those who like stories salted with neat remembrances, Leo's successor was Keith Jackson, now the heralded television sports announcer for ABC.

So now Leo was gone. Suddenly this man whose voice had shaped the way I saw things was silent—it was like having the plug pulled from a part of your life. The brightness went out of it, not because of Leo's departure, really; but the simple fact of his retirement coincided with my own decision—that writing sports every day wasn't fun any more. Leo symbolized the innocence of years I once loved; that's all it was. "Do you miss sports?" people sometimes ask.

Does a man or a woman miss a marriage that has atrophied in the emptiness of small talk? "What's a bore, darling?" asked that good, that rich bitch in *The Snows of Kilimanjaro*. "Anything you do too bloody long," he said.

6

Long Shot Pete

Thomas Peter Rademacher, otherwise known as Pete, should have been a mayor of Seattle—or at the very least in high councils of city planning. He had a flair for administration and projected goals. He certainly could run the Convention & Visitors Bureau; the World's Fair of 1962 should have used his talent. If Pete Rademacher had lived above the Arctic circle, scarcely an igloo would be without an ice box. Had he lived in the 1920s, a time celebrated as the Era of Wonderful Nonsense, Pete Rademacher would have been enshrined in the pages of Americana—along with the era's fabled flagpole sitters, explorers and swimmers of the English Channel.

Peter was a blood cousin to "Wrong Way" Corrigan, to Gertrude Ederle, to Amelia Earhart, to Admiral Byrd, even to Charles Lindbergh himself. Rademacher was only a prizefighter—an amateur one at that—but he dreamed in bold, imaginative colors and for a few brief weeks in the summer of 1957 Pete gave Seattle a luminous, festive glow that this once-drab city had never enjoyed before.

I first knew Pete when he boxed in the *P–I*'s annual Golden Gloves tournaments of those years. He was a big, broad fellow with a farm boy's innocent countenance—featuring a wide, friendly smile that radiated warmth in his considerable vicinity. Because he was this way—relaxed, open and talkative—few of us were prepared for the canny, Voltairean imagination that lay behind his deceptive front.

All alone, Rademacher lifted Seattle into world prominence with one brief sports event. Pete's dream began to take shape during his army days in Fort Benning, Georgia. It depended on a veritable quinella—indeed, a parlay—of long-shot circumstances for its realization. Pete's plan was to become the recognized amateur heavyweight champion of the world. Then he would challenge the world professional title-holder. As simple as that: amateur vs. professional.

Pete first confided his mad scheme to Mike Jennings, a well-heeled Yale graduate who ran a sporting goods store in Columbus, Georgia. Without the formality of turning professional, Pete explained, he would go after the heavyweight professional title. He would win his amateur qualification bouts in America, go on to Melbourne, Australia, and win his preliminary fights at the 1956 Olympic Games, then become the gold medal winner—a recognized, heavyweight, simon-pure title-holder all over the world. "Pete told me," Jennings recalled later, " 'Maybe I can meet a Russian in the finals and knock his head in.' "

Pete won his qualifying fights, and on the evening of November 30, 1956, he was ready for his next-to-last winning parlay in a design that would shake the country with disbelief.

Six hours before this moment, a youth named Floyd Patterson had knocked out the veteran Archie Moore in Chicago and thus became the world's professional heavyweight champion—a title then vacant because its previous incumbent, Rocky Marciano, had retired to more peaceful pursuits. An hour before the Olympics final in Australia, a Seattleite named George Chemeres, Rademacher's trainer, friend, coach and counselor, put in a call to Melbourne. He wanted to wish his protege good luck.

Chemeres dialed the long-distance operator to place his felicitous message to Rademacher in Australia. "Give me," he instructed, "about twenty dollars worth of that four-dollars-a-minute-time." In a few moments, the air turned blue as Rademacher told his friend, "George, when I win this one, I'm going after Patterson's title. I'll announce it here and you'll handle me in the fight."

"Don't talk crazy!" Chemeres screamed into the phone. "You're out of your mind, don't talk crazy!"

Rademacher's deep laughter came through loud and clear over the long distance line as Chemeres shrieked his protests. "Don't say anything over there," he pleaded. "Stay quiet, don't tell anybody. They'll put you in an Australian bughouse and we'll never see you again!" Rademacher agreed to keep his bizarre announcement quiet and Chemeres, sweating profusely, was faced with $52.80 in telephone charges.

So it was that Rademacher, a short time later, stared at an excessively large Russian youth named Lev Moukhine across a boxing ring in Melbourne. The seminal punch was not long in coming. In the opening seconds of the first round, Rademacher made a left-hand feint, then launched a right-hand punch that, in the words of one American boxing critic, "caressed Moukhine's jaw with the familiar American vigor that foreign boxers seldom seem prepared for." Moukhine landed on the canvas with the dull thud of a Russian Five-Year Plan. He got up three times to absorb more such right hands, but the referee stopped the fight before the first round ended. Rademacher then stood center stage, on the traditional Olympic Games platform, proclaimed as the best amateur heavyweight fighter in the world. Pete was in business.

Pete returned to Columbus, Georgia, to further advance his adventure with Mike Jennings, a wealthy Pittsburgh transplant with bold ideas of his own. Jennings, along with his brother-in-law and several other insiders, set up a corporation known as Youth Unlimited. It was a corporation devoted, they said, to encouraging clean, wholesome, uplifting, spiritual and non-criminal behavior in America's young people. "We expect to make a profit, of course," Jennings said, in case there was any doubt about the implied benevolence of his new company. It was further announced that Pete Rademacher would serve as Youth Unlimited's vice-president at a salary of two hundred dollars a week.

The grandiose nature of Pete's vice-presidential duties were kept secret as the firm began raising capital. Youth Unlimited needed a fat guarantee in order to approach Cus D'Amato, Patterson's manager, who himself harbored strains of Voltaire in his maverick makeup. The firm began raising money among some twenty-two Georgians with a zest for youth improvement, or at least a desire to see a black champion relieved of his title. Pete's plan did not remain secret for long as he began to consult professional boxing people. Chemeres once again implored Pete to "stop talking crazy, you can't do things this way." When Jack Hurley, a renowned professional boxing figure, was told of the scheme, he rasped, "What have you guys been smoking?"

A similar reaction came from D'Amato. Rademacher and Jennings arrived in New York with $100,000 in talking money. D'Amato figuratively showed them the door. The pair went back to their twenty-two Georgian investors and returned again to confront D'Amato. Would he let his champion, Patterson, fight Rademacher for a $250,000 guarantee? Again, D'Amato was dubious, but when they showed him the $250,000, his imagination responded to this shock therapy. The fight was on.

Through all of it, Pete's was the ruling imagination. He decreed that the bout would be held in Seattle where he was well-known, a place he always considered his home town. Pete then hired Hurley at a flat fee of $18,000 to handle promotion of the fight. Chemeres was put in charge of his training. Rademacher, a polished, articulate, college-educated man (he was graduated from Washington State University with a degree in business) sat in on all meetings, all negotiations, with final say on the many details attendant to a large heavyweight championship fight.

Pete held an initial press conference in Georgia. The media began to refer to him as "the pug in the gray flannel suit," and wryly formalized his title with Youth Unlimited as "T. Peter Rademacher, vice-president." Howls of outrage from boxing purists around the nation were not long in coming. But as the crescendo of indignation increased, there was one cool, dissenting voice in the Pacific Northwest—the voice of Royal Brougham, sports editor of the *P–I* and a Sunday school teacher with the instincts of a Barnum. Brougham quickly saw exactly what Rademacher envisioned. This fight would fire everyone's imagination with its improbable grotesquerie and Quixote spirit. In Brougham's reckoning, this heavyweight title fight, the first of its kind ever to be held, would celebrate Seattle and sell papers, two thoughts that never were far from his mind.

I first learned of the fight from Royal, whom Rademacher had consulted in confidence. My own reaction was as knee-jerk as any of the more tradition-bound professionals. I cranked up to write some furious, denunciatory pieces about Pete's design against reason (nothing makes a columnist happier than to find something to be indignant about). It was then I got another of many invaluable lessons from Royal Brougham, a master in the subtle readings of public reaction.

He called me into his office and delivered one of those convoluted lectures he was famous for—full of pauses, slang phrases, half-sentences and sly compliments. I can't reconstruct it from this distance, but the message went something like this:

"Look kid, use your imagination . . . ah, you aren't, I mean . . . ah, dumber than a prizefighter, are you? This, ah . . . well, this thing is going to catch on like a brush fire. This'll be the biggest thing we ever had in this town. You'll, ah . . . have lots of fun writing about this . . . ah, lotta your friends like Red Smith and Jimmy Cannon and that Lardner guy will be here . . . and, ah, you know Jack Hurley's for it. . . ."

Then I called Hurley to get his reaction, which was a bit more profane than Brougham's. "Don't knock the fight," he said, "this'll be a real ball-buster." Hurley was now a convert, having embraced this new, positive view because Rademacher had by now made him a hired hand.

As the promotion—the promulgation of Pete's dream—began to take shape, many prominent figures, in boxing and out of it, continued a clamorous uproar. Julius Helfland, chairman of the New York State Athletic Commission and president of the World Championship Boxing Committee, described himself as "utterly astounded." He fired off a telegram to the president of the National Boxing Association, which said in part: "It is shocking to contemplate the possibility of a rank amateur with no previous professional experience being permitted to contest against the world heavyweight champion. . . . an outrageously impossible and unwarranted contest." Such former champions as Jack Dempsey and Joe Louis joined the chorus of denunciations.

Rep. Hugh Scott, of Pennsylvania, pleaded with Washington's then governor Albert Rosellini "to take immediate steps to cancel the scheduled . . . so-called world championship fight." His wire further implored Rosellini, "Please act to save boxing and elevate television." Since there would be no television coverage anyway, it was a moot point. Television went on in its indubitably low state, unaffected by Pete's dream. Nat Fleischer, boxing's official historian, became so undone that he sent a protesting wire to Washington's "Governor Langley," long since out of office, and misspelling his name to boot. Some protesters urged Rosellini to call out the National Guard, if necessary, to prevent Pete Rademacher from carrying out his devilish plan.

Royal Brougham, having nudged my own mind into a pro-Rademacher groove, assigned me to write a four-part history of the fight, its germination to its conclusion. Because of my friendship with Pete and with Chemeres, I was able to get to Rademacher early, when he secluded himself in a small cabin on the north fork of the Snoqualmie River, just outside North Bend. I was slow to accept the fact that Pete was the real architect of this improbable circus. At first I suspected the Machiavellian handiwork of promoter Jack Hurley, and so did many others. But as we talked on, Rademacher and I alone in the room, it became clear that no ordinary professional could have dreamed up this one. Only a gifted amateur, with much luck, a flair for showmanship and a creative disdain for accepted procedures, could have brought the heavy-weight champion of the world to Seattle to risk his title—a title valued in millions of dollars. Rademacher laughed up-roariously as he told how professionals like Chemeres, Rocky Marciano, Hurley and D'Amato, failed at first to grasp his concept of such a fight. He said all of them had told him that he should "get a few professional fights, get yourself a repu-tation," before challenging tradition. Pete's reply to these objections was one of patient exasperation.

"What they don't see, what they don't understand," he explained, "is that even if I win a whole string of pro fights, I'm still just another pro fighter. This way—coming into it as an amateur—makes all the difference. It makes the fight. That's the nature, the very life, of the idea."

As Pete sat on a sofa in his then-secret living quarters, he took unbridled joy in recounting how he put his plan together. He repeated with delight how "D'Amato went right out of his head," when the full impact of the scheme sunk in. D'Amato, however, regained his senses in time to demand (and get) a $100,000 forfeit bond for a return match—in case the incredible happened.

"He told me," Pete said, unable to suppress his laughter, "that he thought everybody was nice and honest out there in Seattle, but he didn't want any of my friends judging his title away. So we agreed on a nationally-known referee that D'Amato would trust."

D'Amato sent Pete a list of referees and Rademacher, acting as his own agent, agreed on Tommy Loughran, a respected boxing official out of Philadelphia. Rademacher further agreed to the no-judges proviso—"none of my hometown friends," he laughed. Only Loughran, as referee, could determine a winner if the fight went the scheduled course of fifteen rounds. Boxing writers who came to Seattle for the match could not be discouraged in their belief that the sly, cynical Hurley was to blame for what they regarded as the greatest mismatch since Johnstown vs. Flood. They refused to accept the truth—that Rademacher alone was the entrepreneur who drew them to this far corner of the Northwest. Nonetheless, they were impressed (as were wise boxing heads) by Pete's ready grasp of the fight's promotional mechanics.

At press conferences Pete displayed a smooth, vice-presidential posture. "How are you today, gentlemen?" he would ask. "Are you enjoying your stay?" When a skeptical reporter wondered about his B.A. degree from Washington State, Pete replied smoothly: "I started out by majoring in journalism, but I soon found out that was a dead end. So I switched to animal husbandry." Rademacher laughed at efforts of Chemeres and his handlers to edit his newspaper reading, many of the stories being derogatory and sarcastic. "They even clipped out 'Joe Palooka,' " he proclaimed, referring to a wholesome prizefighter in a comic strip of that era. "Is Pete nervous?" I once asked Chemeres. "No, he's not nervous," Chemeres replied. "The man is calmer and smarter than me. Didn't he put me and Hurley back in business?"

Rademacher set up his training headquarters in the Issaquah Fire Department's recreation hall. By now the crowds were increasing at his workouts. Everyone wanted a look at the man who would be king: T. Peter Rademacher, vice-president, boxing division, Youth Unlimited. D'Amato set up his champion's training headquarters near Kent. Newspapermen kept arriving from across the nation. True to Brougham's prediction, Red Smith and his celebrated column arrived from the *New York Herald Tribune*. So did Jimmy Cannon, the florid prose-poet of the *New York Post*, along with Harry Grayson, long a top syndicated sportswriter. Once, when I drove Cannon to Rademacher's camp and took a scenic detour back to Seattle, Jimmy said, "Let's do this again—I'd rather look at those trees than this silly fight." Broadway to the core, Jimmy was amazed that he could find a good steak in an outpost like Seattle. Also arriving were Walt Kelly, the famed creator of the comic strip "Pogo," and John Lardner, on assignment from the *New Yorker* and *Newsweek*. Others came from Chicago, Miami, Houston, San Francisco and various parts of Canada. In all, the out-of-town press numbered about one hundred literary stylists.

Meanwhile, at the Olympic Hotel, which housed most of the fight's luminaries, Mike Jennings was holding press conferences. The president of Youth Unlimited was at pains to explain the goals of his corporation, whose principal assets seemed to be Rademacher and a man named Lucky Mc-Daniel, who was marketing a "seeing-eye" BB gun on behalf of the corporation. McDaniel would regularly take reporters out for lessons in his shoot-from-the-hip methods (an early convert was Marty Kane, of *Sports Illustrated*). Since Youth Unlimited was devoted to the betterment of youth, it was Lardner, the gifted miner of irony, who observed that the BB gun, if marketed properly among youth, would eliminate the switch-blade knife, "and revolutionize juvenile delinquency."

Jennings had a lot of loose ends to tidy up, obvious contradictions to resolve. In one press conference I attended, he explained that Youth Unlimited would invest its profits "in

the things that made America great, like General Motors and
General Electric, the things that really built the country." He
also said, "We are in the business of selling America back to
Americans, and we expect to make a profit doing it."
Lardner, briefly a Harvard man, later remarked, "All those
Yale guys are like that—selling America back to Americans."

Youth Unlimited, Jennings emphasized, was determined
to promote wholesome amateur examples to youth. When
somebody suggested that Patterson was a wholesome youth,
Jennings agreed, saying, "Patterson would be our kind of
man, except for the amateur element." He rattled off the
names of several amateur athletes his group would prefer over
professionals. "This is why Youth Unlimited would prefer a
Rademacher over a Patterson, a Gehrig over a Ruth." Somebody pointed out that the late great Lou Gehrig, for all his
fine qualities, was inescapably a professional. I remember
asking if, since both Lou Gehrig and Babe Ruth were professionals, Youth Unlimited made judgments by other criteria.
Ruth was a notorious drinker, wencher and carouser, but he
was, without question, the greatest sports hero American
youth ever knew up to then. The answer never really came
across, and I remember that Jennings got a bit peevish when
somebody pointed out that Youth Unlimited's first major assault on the uplifting of youth was to turn Rademacher, an
amateur, into a professional.

Elsewhere in the Olympic Hotel, in a room much smaller
than Jennings' suite, Hurley was running his end of the show
off a bedspread. Bills of all denominations were being
counted on the bed, tickets costing twenty dollars each were
stacked on a dresser; drifters, friends, alleged mobsters, sportswriters and gofers made the room a suffocating sauna of
sweat, smoke and loud conversation. Hurley would pause,

occasionally, to launch a diatribe against television and radio demands to carry the fight. There would be, he said, no radio and no television, and he intended to put up a big canvas to prevent "those #$!*!!# freeloaders" from watching the fight. The bout would be held at Sicks' Stadium, Seattle's tidy little minor league ball park in Rainier Valley. The hill back of the left field fence made an ideal haven for freeloaders and radio people determined to bootleg a broadcast of the fight.

It was clear from the beginning that Rademacher's twenty-two Georgia backers figured to lose money. The very logistics of the stadium and the pre-fight ticket sales insured that gate receipts, after deducting taxes, ball park rent, and Hurley's promotional fee, would not cover the guarantee of $250,000 for Patterson. However, the Youth Unlimited officers, plus a contingent of Georgia backers and fans, radiated confidence that a miracle would happen. They were the only ones who did, except for Rademacher himself.

At his Issaquah training headquarters, Pete put out daily bulletins which bristled with confidence. "I'm an amateur only by label," Rademacher would say. "I've trained like a pro, I fight like a pro, and I think like a pro. I'm quick to learn and what I learn I can apply." Rademacher gave much credit to his teacher and friend, George Chemeres, along with Joe Gannon, his trainer, a former light heavyweight contender, who was Rademacher's buddy in the army. At one point, Rademacher held up one of his large broad hands. "I won't be afraid," he said. "I've never been afraid in the ring. I am big, I am strong, and I have felt men being hurt from the bones in my fist. And Patterson is only a man."

Pete's confidence, eloquently expressed, made for excellent copy. His vice-presidential demeanor, his flowing, articulate sentences captivated wordsmiths, who poured out reams of copy about the audacity of his plan. If publicity waned for a day, there was always something else. A great to-do was made of photographic copies of the $250,000 cashier's check, put in a downtown bank, to insure that Rademacher had produced his guarantee. Pictures of the check appeared in the papers and were sent by wirephoto across the country.

I got a tip that Tommy Loughran, the referee, had just arrived. It seems improbable now, but even with a horde of competing press in town, I found Loughran alone and very talkative in his hotel room.

"Nothing," he said, "nothing short of a knockout will make me stop this fight. It will be a fight to the finish! There will be no technical knockout. The bout will either go to a decision or when one man is prone on the floor." Loughran's testimony was all the more surprising since he had long been known, in his prizefighting days, as a gentlemanly fellow with Philadelphia social connections. His earnestness in projecting a possible bloodbath, one that he could countenance as the bout's sole official, added to the pre-fight hullabaloo. Loughran clearly had rehearsed his lines with Hurley, whose own zeal now matched that of Rademacher.

Patterson sparred in a ring set up on the Kent Junior High School tennis courts. Mike Donohoe, one of the best friends I ever had in the newspaper business, quarterbacked the coverage. Dick Sharp, the *P-I*'s veteran boxing writer, worked both the Rademacher and Patterson camps. He alternated with a young kid lately out of Yakima, who had joined the *P-I* sports desk a year before. The young kid was John Owen, who eventually succeeded Royal Brougham as the paper's star sportswriting attraction.

Since I was doing columns as well as features on the fight, Donohoe gave me what might be called floating privileges. "Just go out and find all the stuff you can on this daffy show," he instructed. So on the Sunday before the fight I went out to one of Patterson's workouts. It was an excessively hot day. After going a few rounds with a couple of sparmates, Patterson settled in to cool off, using a house trailer that had been set up on the school grounds for his dressing room. Only three or four writers were on hand as Patterson followed the pre-fight code then in vogue of speaking well of your opponent. He praised Rademacher as a boxer, said he liked the people in the Northwest, and predicted a difficult fight for himself. In a moment, the festive atmosphere of the interview changed. A newspaper man from Columbus, Georgia, who had widely predicted a Rademacher victory, injected a dark note into the conversation:

"I wish you were making this fight down in Columbus, boy." Patterson stiffened, but kept his poise. "Yes?" he said, politely. The Columbus man, who clearly had obtained access to a few cans of beer, then began kidding the champion. His Southern drawl was drenched with condescension. When a camp handler gave Patterson a cup of tea, the Georgian said, "You're going to drink tea. Just a nice cup of tea? Why do you drink tea?"

Patterson's head turned and he glared at the Georgian with hostility. "Because I don't like coffee," he said, evenly. From that moment on, I began to see the fight in a much different context. It was all fun up to now, the whole crazy business, with its amateur ideals, its seeing-eye BB guns, its smooth-talking vice-presidential challenger, and Youth Unlimited's goal of "setting examples to sell the youth on America."

That night I had dinner with Lardner and Kelly. I told them what I'd seen and heard. It was a reminder that the fight, inescapably, was a Georgia production, in which Rademacher seemed to encounter no trouble in finding the Dixie banknotes to make his challenge for a black man's title. Rademacher himself was obviously an enlightened guy in such matters. So, probably, were Mike Jennings and other corporate officers of Youth Unlimited. At least they were at pains to speak of the champion in only the most glowing terms. But it also seemed clear—if anyone forgot the three-ring circus flavor of the fight itself—that others, with less lofty motivations, were willing to put up cash in hopes of seeing a Nordic, like Rademacher, defeat Patterson.

Whatever these suspicions, and they were never voiced publicly, it seemed prudent to at least ask Patterson for his views. I drove out to Patterson's quarters on Star Lake with Lardner and Kelly. Patterson lived in a small lakeside cottage with his retinue of handlers. It was a lovely, warm summer afternoon, some thirty hours before the fight, and Patterson was out taking a walk. His manager, Cus D'Amato, had journeyed into town on some business errand, possibly to take a final, reassuring look at Youth Unlimited's $250,000 check. Patterson returned from his walk wearing heavy outdoor boots, denim pants and a light gray shirt. Before we went in, I told Lardner, "I'm going to ask him the White Hope question." Lardner nodded and we all sat down in the small living room. With D'Amato absent, Patterson could clearly express his own views without managerial censorship.

Patterson talked the trivia of the fight. Yes, he felt fine, yes, he thought Rademacher was a worthy opponent, yes, his weight was about right. And so forth. Then I asked Floyd if there was anything about the fight that troubled him. "What do you mean?" he asked. I said, "I was wondering if you had any feeling that this fight had a White Hope element in it?" For some sixty years, White Hopes were what Caucasians looked for whenever a black man held the heavyweight title.

As Patterson began to speak, his words betrayed a private anger he seemed to have suppressed for days; he appeared genuinely relieved that a group of friendly questioners had brought up the subject. "I definitely think this is a White Hope fight," he said. "If I had been a white fighter, they never would have put up any $250,000 for this fight. In New York they couldn't have raised $250 for this kind of fight."

Patterson spoke slowly, searching carefully for the correct words to express his disgust and anger. His voice was full of bitterness and he appeared eager to get his thoughts on record. "These people are playing on my mind, like they know it must be weak," Patterson said. "I hear I'll be knocked out in two rounds, three rounds. Maybe in a room Rademacher could take away my title, selling me."

I brought up the incident involving the Columbus man, who had chided him about drinking tea, the man who had called him "boy." "It wasn't just that one man," he said. "They've been getting more messages to me. They talk like I was a different kind of person, something lower down." His handlers seemed to approve what Floyd was saying, an indication that here at least, in his own camp, they had reason to believe their champion was being downgraded and cheapened.

"If the money could be raised anywhere but Georgia," Patterson continued, referring to the celebrated $250,000 guarantee, "why couldn't they raise it here, in his home territory? I'm asked will I carry him?" he concluded. "Would Pete carry me? What would they say to him in Georgia if he carried me?

This fight leaves a bad taste in my mouth. Louis had one like it with Schmeling. I never wanted to win one more in my life."

The interview ended, finally, and Patterson went around shaking hands, seeming relieved that he had somehow purged himself. "Thanks," he said, as in "thanks for listening." As we drove back to Seattle, the notion occurred that I was the only daily newspaperman to have heard all this. Lardner's stuff would not appear for a week; Kelly, the cartoonist, was along as a bemused kibitzer. "Lord," I remember thinking, "a hundred newspapermen covering this fight and I've got a story that will blow it out of the water."

I wrote it as a straight news story, no embellishments; with the explosive nature of Patterson's feelings, no embellishments were needed. Donohoe looked up from the first takes and asked, "What are you trying to do, start a race riot?" I just laughed and went on writing. Royal Brougham, getting wind of the story, stopped by to ask if I could verify my quotes. I said yes—that with John Lardner, the best sportswriter in the world, taking the same notes I took—the story could be verified. I finished the piece and went across the street to the New Grove for a drink. Visions of headlines danced in my head; all those big-time writers, and I had scooped them with a blockbuster story.

Then Mike Donohoe came in and found me at the bar. "We aren't going to run your story," he said. "Colvin says he doesn't want a riot on his conscience." Mike referred to Ray Colvin, a frail, sallow-faced night managing editor, whom I liked very much. "Colvin says the goddamned story could touch off some real trouble, and I kind of agree with him. Anyway, the story is killed."

I would like to tell you that I flew into a righteous rage, that I went across the street and threatened to quit on principle if they spiked my story. I did go back to see Ray Colvin. He affirmed his belief that the *P–I* should not be responsible for causing ugly incidents with a story like that. To be honest, I felt a sense of relief that the story would not run. There would be denials, of course; D'Amato would deny everything on behalf of Patterson. With a story like that, and no matter how many witnesses you have, you'd still be in the position of explaining how it all came about. Skeptical colleagues, who do not like to be scooped, would be of little help. Only the denials would get big play. So I was relieved, knowing that when the ringside was jammed before the fight, I wouldn't be the center of disbelieving—even hostile—attention.

As dusk came on the evening of August 22, Jack Hurley ordered the canvas to be hung above the left field fence to stymie freeloaders and bootlegged radio broadcasts. "There ain't enough canvas to swing it on such short notice," he was told by an errand-runner. "Okay," rasped Hurley, "then get the lights going." A series of high-powered spotlights, the kind used at supermarket openings and movie premieres, was trained on the hill across Empire Way, beyond the ball park fence, where several hundred freeloaders had gathered. One story had it that a man became so enraged at being blinded by the spotlights during the fight that he ran home and brought back a .22 rifle to shoot out the bulbs. No shots were fired, however, so cooler heads must have prevailed.

As it turned out, only KING radio, among the broadcasting stations, translated its sullenness into mutiny. Defying Hurley's no-broadcast posture, the station set up its broadcasting nest on the hill. Bill O'Mara was KING's kingpin announcer in those days, and he stationed himself, with a tape recorder and binoculars, in full view of the proceedings. Later the program director was heard to say, "If the fight had gone a couple more rounds, poor Bill would have been blind." Today, Bill O'Mara can only laugh at the whole business. "I was so blinded by the spots that I couldn't tell which color the fighters were." But O'Mara was able to piece together a delayed broadcast of the bout, adding one more sideshow to what went on inside the main tent.

A long delay after preliminary bouts held up the main event. Rademacher was first to climb into the ring, ready to perform his vice-presidential duties on behalf of Youth Unlimited. One of Pete's remarks stuck in my mind: "If you're going into a business, you might as well start at the top." Royal Brougham was sitting next to me and he leaned forward to confide: "You know it's all been fun up to now, but I'm not sure I want to see what happens next." Patterson, exercising a champion's prerogative, took his own time about coming into the ring. The crowd of 16,961 was mostly good-natured, but grew impatient at Patterson's delay.

"Maybe the check bounced, Pete!" yelled a man in the rear.

Patterson was a quick hitter who tended to attack in flurries. Rademacher, wisely counseled by Chemeres, crowded the smaller man, using his weight and strength to keep Patterson off-balance. Pete landed several blows to the head; they were not solid blows but they annoyed Patterson, who tried to strike back in rapid bursts of punching. In the second round, a fight that many regarded as the epitome of nonsense was anything but nonsense. Rademacher caught the champion with a straight left, then got in a strong right hand to Patterson's left cheek. The blow sent Patterson down (he may have slipped, but he was definitely down) and the count went to three before the champion got up, obviously with his skull buzzing. At round's end, he returned to his corner, looking a bit sheepish. As D'Amato brought the champ's stool to his corner, he grinned the way a father grins when his child disobeys orders and falls into trouble. "See what I told you?" he seemed to be saying.

For whatever reason, Rademacher let up on his crowding tactics in the third round. This enabled Patterson to attack in rushing flurries. He finally struck Pete the way Churchill wanted to attack the Axis, through the soft underbelly of Europe. He hit Rademacher in the stomach. Then he knocked Pete down with a punch to the jaw. Then began, as someone pointed out, eighteen of the most painful minutes ever endured by a vice-president in the line of corporate duty. T. Peter Rademacher went down five more times, each for a count of nine. Referee Tommy Loughran, true to his Darwinian pledge that only the fittest would emerge from the abattoir, refused to stop the fight. It went on until the sixth round when, to the vast relief of everyone, including even Patterson, Pete stayed down for the full count of ten. In all, Loughran had pumped his arm sixty-four times over a prone vice-president, who later issued a business-like statement from his dressing room: "I'm pleased to have fought the champion. I found him exceedingly strong, exceedingly quick, and exceedingly fair."

It was a statement worthy of a corporation devoted to the betterment of youth. The adventure left Youth Unlimited with a mixed bag of results. Its vice-president had lost, so there went a chance for personal appearances, Rademacher T-shirts, Rademacher lectures, Rademacher-endorsed sporting equipment, plus the chance for another (and perhaps more lucrative) Rademacher fight. But at least the Dixie corporation got its vice-president out of town in one piece. It had weakened its amateur cause by turning an amateur into a professional. But it benefitted a youth—Patterson, age twenty-two—with a bequest of $250,000. And it unavoidably enriched the life of Jack Hurley, a professional promoter who hated amateurs. Mr. Hurley was later heard to confess in an unguarded moment, "Imagine that—an amateur did this for me. I guess there is some good in everybody." Youth Unlimited lost a total of $125,000, which doesn't seem like a lot if your competitive field is selling youth on America.

From a distance of twenty-five years, the whole event seems a trifle unreal. Patterson's brief, bitter outburst notwithstanding, no city ever was treated to such a joyous, implausible spectacle; for a few brief days, the Era of Wonderful Nonsense returned. The bout may have proved, if it proved anything at all, that Floyd Patterson never was a great champion; he lacked the size and the punch to be one. A really good puncher would never have taken seven knockdowns to finish Rademacher. Floyd is a fine, thoughtful man, a man of sensitivity and dignity. One of the saddest stories I ever read in sports was an account of how Muhammad Ali stripped away this dignity by calling him "the rabbit," and proclaiming to the world that Patterson really was the white man's plaything. To me, Floyd was a man of profound dignity and pride that day in his cabin on Star Lake; he felt degraded and he wanted to get his thoughts on record.

In the ensuing years Patterson broke away from Cus D'Amato. He was destroyed by the likes of Sonny Liston and Muhammad Ali; he engaged in a number of losing, disappointing fights that must have wiped from his memory any bad feelings he may have had about Seattle and Pete Rademacher.

As for Rademacher, he is no longer the vice-president of

anything. Following the one fight which made him truly famous, Pete went on fighting for a few years, piling up a record of seventeen victories, six losses and one draw. He never had a manager or a trainer; he picked up his corner handlers when he came into a town. He wasn't all fluff, bluff and salesmanship. He fought a number of respectable heavyweights, beating such as Willy Besmenoff and George Chuvalo, the Canadian champion. In his biggest payday, Pete got $38,000 for fighting a top-ranked heavyweight named Zora Folley. He got his clock cleaned. Pete's final professional fight came on April 4, 1962, when he whipped "Bobo" Olsen, the former middleweight champion. This was in Honolulu and the next day, sunning on the sand at Waikiki Beach, he determined to call it a career.

Youth Unlimited dissolved shortly after its singular venture in Seattle. Mike Jennings left Georgia and now lives in Florida. In addition to his fighting, Pete booked and promoted for Lucky McDaniel, the BB gun wizard. He tried a number of business ventures and made a comfortable living. He sold houses, hustled IBM equipment, trained fighters and promoted a few boxing shows. In one of his last boxing ventures, Pete acted as matchmaker for a fight card in Columbus. He promoted the show, signed all the fighters, handled the publicity, sold advance tickets, refereed two of the preliminary bouts, then climbed into the ring himself—to fight the main event. Clearly, a man for all seasons.

He is, as I said, no longer the vice-president of anything. For the past twelve years he has been an executive with Kiefer-McNeil, a division of the large, diversified McNeil Corporation, based in Akron, Ohio. Kiefer-McNeil has supplied swimming and training equipment for the past three Olympic Games and will do so again in the 1984 Olympics at

Los Angeles. You will find Pete Rademacher today in Medina, Ohio. On his desk is a plaque which reads: "T. Peter Rademacher, President."

I had to ask him: "Pete, what if the incredible had happened? What if you had kept Patterson down that night in Seattle?" The laughter came rolling out of his huge chest. "To tell you the truth," he said, "I'd never have fought again. I'd have milked that title all the way to the bank."

7

Reasonably Honest Jack

A few days after I mislaid the last will and testament of John Cornelius Hurley, I went over to see him in his living room, which was the lobby of the Olympic Hotel. Hurley was a tall, thin-faced, sallow individual who used to thrash around in that living room like a crotchety old uncle, living out his days the way many old folks do, reveling in his ailments, repeating stories of past glories, and calling upon heavenly witnesses to observe how he had to suffer the company of fools. His hypochondriacal hyperbole often made good copy, but he didn't stop at newspapermen. He would regale helpless listeners (often bewildered hotel guests) with a litany of physical ailments that would exceed the listings found in a medical student's textbook.

He repeatedly said he had only two-thirds of a stomach, the other third having been stolen from him by some plumber posing as a doctor. His rectal operations, he said, did nothing to relieve his pain in that region. He claimed a record number of sinus operations (twenty-four), was bereft of his tonsils, his appendix and his respect for the American medical system. "After twenty-four sinus operations they said you don't need 'em,'' he would complain. "But I guarantee you, let them find a new disease and I will have it the next day.''

Anyway, I had lost his will. The way I had lost his will is that, through some extraordinary set of meaningless circumstances, I ended up as the will's executor. It developed somewhat earlier that Hurley, having made out his will, entrusted its execution to an old pan game dealer he knew down on Third Ave. The legal work he left with an uptown attorney. Then one day, as the attorney described the scene, Hurley rushed up to him on the street in an advanced state of indignation.

"That guy died,'' Hurley announced, in a tone that implied the man's personal betrayal of his interests.

The attorney tried to soothe Hurley. "Don't worry about it, Jack,'' he said. "I can take care of things out of my office.''

Hurley stepped back and surveyed his lawyer. "You don't look so good yourself,'' he said, dubiously. "I think we better go find another executor.''

So after mulling over a few names, then rejecting them, they settled on me. This was in 1965, and Hurley called to break the news. "Now I don't want you to write this and make a big deal out of it, but you are my new executor.'' I said I was honored, kind of. He said, "The reason I picked you is that I think you are too dumb to be larcenous.'' With that tribute ringing in my ears, I called the lawyer to learn the precise duties of an executor. "Well, your first duty,'' he said, "is to outlive Hurley.''

The only other duty, it seemed, was to hang onto the will

and keep it a secret until such time as Hurley went to that Great Boxing Hippodrome in the Sky. And now I had lost it. To keep the younger generation from asking silly questions, let us here reveal that Deacon Jack Hurley was a fight manager and promoter. He had made and lost several modest fortunes managing fighters and promoting matches in Fargo, North Dakota, Chicago and Seattle. He frequently promoted for fighters he also managed, which is not nice and sometimes illegal. At the time I lost his will, I guessed he had sizable sums stashed in safety deposit boxes, a couple of banks and in something in the Olympic Hotel safe he called "my lard can."

On this day when I showed up in his living room to confess my shoddy neglect of his touching trust in my honesty, the Deacon was seventy-four years old. The first news when we shook hands was good, because Hurley instantly began complaining about his physical welfare. This always was believed, especially among sportswriters, to be a sign of good health in Jack. When he was in good shape he would complain; when he was sick he would keep quiet about it.

"I feel terrible," the Deacon said, although he usually pronounced it "turrible." But this time he was on the money. "Terrible, never felt worse in my life. Don't see how I can make it much longer." He held his suit coat open. "As you can see, I'm wearing my 'planting suit,' so as to be ready. I always buy dark suits these days to be buried in. I feel rotten."

"That gives me more time to find your will," I said.

Hurley stood back, genuinely startled. "What did you do with it, where is it?" he demanded.

"It's around someplace," I hedged. I said my office had been moved to another part of the building, so the will may have slipped down into a crack or got misfiled under "stories to write later."

Instead of exploding into anger, he said, "Well, you better find it, because I got a feeling we ain't got much time. I feel turrible." I edged the conversation away from his mislaid will to a topic I was sure would set him off on new flights of indignation. "How many people do you think might anticipate your demise with pleasure?" I asked.

"I wouldn't want to guess," he said. "We'd need a computer to count 'em. It doesn't matter anyway. My ambition is to check out with a draw. I want to go not owing anybody and having no money left to give anybody. That's another thing. I've already given my business to Wilbur Lewis, the undertaker. He's a former boxing commissioner and he never ruled against me, so I figure he's all right. I want to be buried in Fargo. I already paid for the lot. I already paid for the casket, too, so I want you to be sure they don't switch in a cheap casket on me."

The Deacon said it cost him $1,000 a month to live. "And I don't live high," he added. "I got to have eating money and I got to have sleeping money. I'll never manage another fighter, but I might do some promoting." Just as a conversational diversion, I asked him if he ever sat up late and watched television. For much of his life he had scorned and denounced television as "the ruination of boxing. You give it away to freeloaders and they won't buy tickets." This was before the days when fighters and managers and promoters reaped extravagant sums from television revenue. Not even that question touched him off. "Sometimes I sit up and watch TV," he admitted. "After all it *is* free, and I figure I'm losing money if I don't watch it."

It was sad, in a way, to see the old guy, playing out obsolete jokes on a new situation. There was a strain of truth in his mournful litany. He had lived out his life, his glory days were over, and like an aging vaudevillian he was trying to pump new energy into old routines before the hook pulled him off the stage. But there was a day . . .

Hurley first hit Seattle in 1950. For a long time, University of Washington football not excepted, he was the biggest running sports story in town. If there was no news he would create some, being very wily, quite greedy, and fully attuned to what made a story, an angle, a good picture and even a headline. He had taken up a local fighter, Harry Matthews, a run-of-the-mill middleweight, whom he blew up into a light heavyweight. When he saw that the light heavyweight division was too formidable for Matthews (Archie Moore and Joey Maxim were two of the more gifted activists in that weight class) he loudly announced that all such title contenders "are afraid of my athlete. I will now campaign Matthews as a heavyweight."

Matthews was what the trade called a "stab, grab and apologize" fighter for most of his career. What Hurley did was put weight on him, slow him down, teach him the art of slipping and counter-punching, and skillfully build him up as a strictly Northwest attraction. He made a sizable fortune doing this. Incredibly, he got Matthews a New York fight with the soon-to-be champion, Rocky Marciano, who dispatched Matthews in the second round. Did he defend his fighter publicly? "He turned amateur on me," rasped the Deacon. Not long after, Matthews retired without consulting Hurley and the Deacon responded in outraged fury. "He is an ingrate. Giving money to a fighter is like putting silk stockings on a pig." He had other fighters, whose names scarcely matter now, but for twelve or fifteen years he played his obbligato on a willing Northwest press.

All columnists sought him out and I was the worst offender. In return, Hurley made me quite well known across the country. This came from his practice of buying a hundred or more papers in which "press notices" appeared about him. He would then laboriously clip them, address envelopes on a battered old typewriter he owned, and mail them to sports desks all over the country. It was the next best thing to being syndicated. I was such an offender in repetitious writing about Hurley that he would beg me not to write anything about him in the Sunday paper. "They cost too much on Sunday," he would complain.

I saw a lot of him during those years. I worked late hours and Von's, a fine old restaurant on Fourth Ave., next to where Pay 'n Save is now, was open twenty-four hours a day. You could usually find the Deacon in a booth with George Chemeres, Bob Wark, Bill Ross and other fight figures. Except for the Olympic's coffee shop, he ate all his meals at Von's. Frequently he sat on the last stool of a long counter next to the kitchen, and Von's owner, Cliff Warling, had his stool inscribed with a bronze plate, "This Stool Reserved for Jack Hurley."

He did some drinking in those days. Sometimes with Chemeres we would drive to some after-hours spot out near Longacres or another deadfall that thrived for a time just past Lake City on old Bothell Way. He drank fast and held it well. Occasionally, when it would get the best of him, he would reveal some details of what he called his "swindles" of the past, and one night he outlined his grandiose plan for getting a fight for Matthews with Jersey Joe Walcott. I forget the exact script but it involved the crudest kind of dump, with the inevitable rematch, and it was designed, he said, to get control of the heavyweight title—keeping it away from the

New York boxing monopoly which Hurley hated, and which always controlled it. Knowing all this, I suppose I should have been chastised by the *Columbia Journalism Review* for not printing such stories. To hell with them then, and to hell with them now. Hurley was too rich a source of endless stories to betray him and shut off the supply.

To be quite honest about it, I owed a lot to the Deacon. I must have peddled a half-dozen magazine stories about him, which added up to enough dough to get my older daughter through college. Anyway, we drank a lot of Scotch together, which always made me suspicious of his story about having only two-thirds of a stomach. No matter how late we stayed out, he always insisted that I drop him off at Von's, where he picked up a single banana and a quart of milk. Once I drove around the block to check on him—he was weaving badly— and I found him walking up Fourth Ave. toward the Olympic, carrying his banana and milk up to his lonely hotel room. In one pocket, I knew, he carried a gun. Because of his "profession," as he called it, Hurley always lived on the edge of the underworld; any serious figure in boxing did in those days. He had a permit to carry the gun, because there had been some threats on his life. "Ain't this a bitch," he once said, showing me the small pistol, "when an honest man has to carry one of these? This used to be an honorable profession, but now it's turrible."

Boxing never was an honorable anything, not even a sport. It was one of Hurley's engaging sophistries to claim any such respectability for it. Boxing was and is a game of angles and fixes, bribes and duplicity, but for anyone who is fascinated by evil, as I am, it is one of the best shows that free enterprise presents. Hurley was a consummate con artist. To this day— notwithstanding those tales prompted by alcohol—I cannot say he ever swindled anybody directly. Probably he did, since boxing thrives on swindle. But in the art of near-larceny, he was a master. He was a virtuoso in subtly presenting fragments of facts, or truth, in his favor; he could drive a swift and savage bargain when he had the upper hand. His persuasion could be overpowering and to suggest he was a con artist is only to say he orchestrated those qualities possessed by some actors and all salesmen.

It was difficult to sift the things he believed from the things he just said he believed, or the things he came to believe because he said them so often. Like most good con artists, Hurley frequently convinced himself. When he was maneuvering Harry Matthews into a big money match with Rocky Marciano, he loudly proclaimed that Marciano was a "turrible boxer," that he was, by the testimony of several unnamed boxing experts, a crude bum who could be taken out by a skilled boxer. The Deacon played this tune so long that it's possible he came to believe the impossible—that Matthews, an inflated middleweight, weighing scarcely 178 pounds, could have stood up to the raging bull that Marciano was. Later, after Matthews was knocked out by Marciano, Hurley began confiding that he had bet $10,000 at big odds on Matthews. This could have been true, but I doubt it. The Deacon did not bleed enough for a man who lost $10,000.

"Amateurs" and "incompetents" were ruining his once "honorable profession," he would insist; "amateurs" and "incompetents" often turned out to be people who simply disagreed with him. This was Hurley, lending a certain elegance to sophistry. His "profession" was in reality a corner, or segment, he staked out in the free enterprise system. It is what much of American business would become if the normal strictures of common humanity were not placed on it. Boxing, as it existed in Hurley's heyday, was simply free enterprise untroubled by rules of law. Anyone who regards this as an extreme comparison is hereby invited to reflect on the powerful interests that were brought to bear against the abolishment of child labor not so many years ago. Whenever I hear the bleats from businessmen and politicians that America is best served by "taking the shackles of regulation" off industry, I always think of boxing and Jack Hurley.

So he staked out an unregulated corner of the free enterprise system. Profit was his sole motive, and in his own tiny, private world he raised free enterprise to an art form. He played his own ruggedly individualistic game, and, while he may not have been precisely what Adam Smith had in mind, Hurley was awfully damned good at capitalism on a small scale. The rest of it was all show. To kill time, he played bridge with the ladies at the Olympic. He played the role of the hypochondriac, the wry jokesmith, the dyspeptic critic-at-large. He did this, I suppose, out of ego or boredom, and for perhaps the same reasons that Barrymore played buffoons and Lawrence Tibbet sang with the "Hit Parade." On the topic of women, he may even have had the con man's foresight of a good thing, a new tune to play, before women began to assert their rights. He got much mileage out of denouncing "the little creatures," and managed to convey an air of genuine concern over all the misery Adam had created with only one rib.

He never was more fascinating than when he could gull writers into giving him publicity against their will. Or when he could bamboozle large sections of the press with a scheme we were too dense to perceive as sheer scam. He reached his height when he worked as the paid promoter for the heavy-

weight championship fight between Pete Rademacher and
Floyd Patterson. The Deacon sent out customary notices to
newspapers across the country, notices on how and where to
apply for ringside seats. Nobody was more aware than Hurley
that the whole idea was bizarre, that it was being loudly criti-
cized as an offense against piety in more solemn segments of
the national sporting press. So with the application forms,
Hurley enclosed a proviso that requests for tickets would be
granted, "only if accompanied by one favorable mention of
the fight." Allegedly sophisticated sportswriters, falling for
this ruse, erupted in printed denunciations all over the
country, thus giving Hurley more attention and publicity
than he otherwise deserved.

But at bottom he genuinely liked people, at least certain
kinds of people. He took an interest in waitresses, doormen,
cops, cab drivers and working stiffs. He often fed them at
Von's or loaned them money out of his "lard can." He lived
a lonely, nocturnal life and such people made up what family
he had in Seattle. His word was always good. He was strident,
impossible, funny, vindictive, tough and difficult. Only
those with a wish to be bamboozled will remember him for
the often folksy role he played.

Early in December, 1971, I got one of Hurley's letters on
Olympic Hotel stationery. In it was an advertisement for a
funeral home, and across the ad he had scratched the nota-
tion, "Just to remind you." Perhaps he had a premonition,
because a few nights later he died in his hotel room, the small
room he slept and worked in for so many years. I don't know
if he was wearing his 'planting suit,' but I do know he didn't
get a draw. His bills were paid and he had some money left
over. As executor of his will, I had to sign a raft of papers for
the lawyers, and these revealed that he left something in

excess of $100,000, mostly to his brother in Fargo. His brother wrote a nice letter to thank me for signing the papers "and for all the stuff you wrote about Jack." He asked me if I wanted a fee for being the executor of his brother's will, or maybe he would buy me a gift of some kind. After thinking it over, I wrote back and said no. I explained that Jack had always thought of me as an amateur and I didn't want to ruin my standing.

8

"Orange Blossom"

Occasionally I see him around town, this friend I admire so much. He is tall, rather angular, with a slightly hooked nose, thin of face with a wry smile, as though he knows something about the world that the rest of us don't. We occasionally have coffee together and his company is always delightful. He has a sharp, yet subdued sense of humor, plus an inner dignity that is reflected in his bearing. On occasion I drop by the Millionair Club to see him.

The Millionair Club is located down on Western Ave., and each morning, and throughout the day, you see the men— usually men, but some women—idling on the sidewalk exchanging small talk. My friend, whose name is Ron Fagan, and the Millionair Club are part of this city's fabric, a part of it I care deeply about. The club itself would not rank among Seattle's "establishment" charities; it gets no funds from United Way; it accepts no government support or any other tax-based funding. Since its founding in 1921, the Millionair Club has served more than 100,000 free meals annually to the indigent, the sick, the unemployables, the drifters, people down on their luck, or what might be called "industrial drop-outs" from society.

Since 1921, it has found literally thousands of full and part-time jobs for guys on the skids. Many people in Seattle have learned to use the Millionair Club when they need some kind of work done. Whenever I go to a Poncho auction, or some other large "establishment" fund-raiser, the haunting thought of the Millionair Club is always there. These things are worthy, indeed, but one can only wonder what the Mil-lionair Club might be if some of our rich givers would be will-ing to get a little dirt on their shoes when they go in search of tax-free places to put their money.

We often hear the phrase, "only in Seattle," to illustrate that the city is unique in some way. Quite logically, no one would think of naming the Millionair Club as a unique insti-tution, yet it is. To the best of anyone's knowledge, the Mil-lionair Club is the only thing of its kind in America—and I might further submit that the world has produced only a few rare individuals like my friend Ron Fagan, who works there.

The first time my friend Ron Fagan got drunk he was ten or twelve years old, and he isn't sure he got drunk that first time, or whether he just felt the buzz from his first drink. This first drink came about 1925. First drink or first drunk, it scarcely mattered. What mattered was that Ron Fagan had a disease that was not fully recognized at that time. By the time he attended Blessed Sacrament grade school, he was what they would call today a confirmed alcoholic. In his sophomore year at Roosevelt High School Ron Fagan was kicked out for habitual drunkenness. They knew he drank and they found a pint of bootleg liquor in his locker. From there it was down, down, down into the spit, slime, degradation and despair found in the skid road before the skid road became chic Pioneer Square.

Ron Fagan used to hang out along First Ave., where the Prohibition speakeasies flourished, and the skid road itself was also where people went to drink when all booze was illegal. Being a kicked-out sophomore from Roosevelt High presented no problem in getting liquor. A kid like Ron Fagan could usually get in a speakeasy. If not, there was "Russian John," who owned some of the speakeasies, and sold bottles to kids on the side. By the time he was seventeen or eighteen, Fagan was a veteran of skid roads in Seattle, Los Angeles, San Francisco and various parts of Alaska. He drank everything from dubious bootleg booze to raw alcohol to cheap wine and canned heat. He kicked around aimlessly, getting an odd job now and then, and saw the beautiful part of his young life —when he saw it at all—through a steady alcoholic haze.

World War II came to Ron Fagan just as it did to everyone else. The physically disabled were classified 4-F; how they classified a drunk when he was drafted is something I don't know. It scarcely matters. Ron Fagan couldn't sober up long enough to be accepted by the army. "But I remember," he once told me, "that I woke up with a terrific hangover on the day the Japanese bombed Dutch Harbor." He had somehow enlisted in the Alaska National Guard, showing up drunk the first day. "That was the day after I hit all the bars on Fourth Street in Anchorage," he says. Later, he managed to get into the Merchant Marine, a tour of duty that saw him end up drunk and broke on the skid road of Manila, where, in those terrible days, one got no lower.

I have asked Ron Fagan several times how he survived. He

doesn't really have a clear answer, but it seems like a miracle today that he is alive. Constantly drunk, he walked the streets of this dangerous section of Manila fully armed. He had a knife tucked up in his sleeve and a .45 calibre revolver tucked in his belt. He cadged drinks, he threatened for drinks; he walked in a lawless nether world, drunk and dangerous and vulnerable. For two years after that, he stayed drunk almost constantly, drifting back to San Francisco and then Seattle. He was now thirty-six. By all measurement guides to anyone's lifetime, his own life had been squandered. He was finished, and he would be a public charge, buffeted about, homeless, friendless and done for. He was an outcast, a wasted failure, approaching middle age; no job, no prospects, no future. He was a reviled specimen in a society that viewed alcoholism not as a disease, but as a weakness, a society which judged such specimens as having nothing more than a flawed moral character.

It is common among those who quit drinking—the hard, recidivist boozers—that they can remember the exact time of their last drink. Some can remember it to the day, the date and the hour, the way some people can remember leaving the scene of a bad accident. Ron Fagan was too far gone to remember the exact date or time, but he does remember the year and the circumstances.

He had been hauled before a Seattle police judge, John Neergaard, in 1947. Judge Neergaard was exasperated beyond patience because of the usual charge: public drunkenness. Neergaard, Fagan remembers, berated him from the bench. "The next time you appear in this courtroom, I'll have you declared a common drunk." The distinction, considering the record of arrests, seemed to be a fine one, since Fagan, by all definitions, already was a common drunk.

It is the nature of the alcoholic that he is not only cunning with others, but cunningly deceptive with himself. He is the last to admit his own problem. Many experts contend that it's the nature of the disease that the victim has to hit bottom before he will admit he needs help. To an alcoholic it is always he or she who is being put upon. The world is against them. People don't understand. Me a drunk? Hell, I can take it or leave it alone.

So to Ron Fagan, the brand, "common drunk," was an insult. No matter how low he was, even then he could not see himself in that category. So he got angry. He remembers muttering under his breath to Judge Neergaard, "I'll show you, you son of a bitch." He left the courtroom and walked down to a place then known as the "Yesler Rehab," and for the second time that day he got angry. "I ran into an old drinking buddy I knew," he recalls. "He was a guy I didn't like much. He told me he'd been ten days without a drink." This fact, the fact of a fellow drunk's sobriety, is what made him sore. "If that bastard can do it," he remembers thinking, "so can I."

Ron Fagan has not had a drink to this day.

If that is all there was to it, we would have a dandy episode to illustrate that man can, indeed, survive. But if that is all there was to it, I would not have been drawn to Ron Fagan the way I am. As I said, Ron Fagan has become a valued friend. We see each other now and then, but by no means does Ron Fagan need to seek out friends. He would be welcome in the Governor's Mansion tomorrow. The doors of any city or state agency, any school or university would be open to this one-time derelict. He has thousands of friends all over Seattle, but it was a long road to that kind of acceptance.

It took Ron Fagan perhaps thirty days to really get sober

after his final drink. It usually takes that long to get the alcohol out of the system of a heavy drinker. For a while, in those days, he lived in a fifteen-cent bed in the old Lucky Flophouse, located at what is now known as Occidental Square. He had no money. He had no skills, but even if he had them, nobody, knowing his background, would have hired him. So he hit for Alaska where he was not so well known and landed in Cordova. This is the part you might think is being made up: he got a job as a bartender, of all things. He worked in a saloon filled with the kind of drinkers only Alaska can produce.

The steady drinkers in his saloon fastened Ron Fagan with the name of "Orange Blossom." This was because when the steady drinkers "bought one for the bartender" the only drink Ron Fagan would accept was orange pop. A more unlikely place to quit drinking, to begin rehabilitating yourself, can scarcely be imagined. But "Orange Blossom" survived.

Later, with a few bucks saved up, Ron Fagan came back to Seattle. "I guess it was more out of curiosity," he once told me, "but I went out to visit the old Seattle Police Rehabilitation Program for Alcoholics, out at the south end of Boeing Field's main runway." He laughs now at the amazement of the police. They were genuinely astonished that Ron Fagan could be sober, much less stay sober. He became, in a way, a sort of police talisman and curiosity.

So they gave him a job by hiding him in their limited budget. He was paid under the designation of "facility baker," but his real job was counseling the endless supply of recidivist alcoholics who came through. He was a good counselor, as it happened, because Ron Fagan spoke the language of drunks, he knew the nuances of their cunning and excuses;

he had learned a lot about the dangerous business of consuming booze.

At one point, an assistant chief asked him, "Ron, how many times have you been arrested?" Fagan shrugged, having no idea. "Okay, we'll check it out," said the assistant chief. His partial arrest record showed that, at one point in his existence, Ron Fagan had been arrested twenty-four times in twenty months. Still hidden in the budget as a "facility baker," he went on working with alcoholics at the rehabilitation center. "Now I had a new problem," he told me. "You see, I was working with my kind of people, the alkies, but I also was working with young medical students. They were about what we had in those days. I found they were talking in a foreign language, using technical and medical terms I couldn't understand."

Which is why Ron Fagan went back to school at the age of thirty-seven. He went to Seattle University—to get his high school diploma. This came hard because the habits of study—which he never really acquired as a young alcoholic at Roosevelt High—had to be mastered. But he made it, and then Ron Fagan decided to go for the big casino—a college degree. By this time he was married, with children, but he stayed on at Seattle U, studying nights, working days, to support his family. Most college freshmen worry about fraternities, how to space the easy and tough courses, where to park, who they can date, as they go through a mildly painful period of adjustment. Ron Fagan had another worry.

"At first I was terribly frightened," he told me one day. "You see, I had been a boozer all my life. In my day, I had drunk so much rotten wine, raw alcohol and canned heat that I was afraid I might have permanently injured my brain. I was terrified that my brain had been addled too much to handle the tough courses in higher education."

It took a long time. Seven years. But in 1960 Ron Fagan was graduated from Seattle University with a B.A. in behavioral sciences, with an emphasis on studies in alcoholism. He did come up short on graduation. On the grade-point scale he was .05 short.

Given that extra .05 on the grade point scale, Ron Fagan would have graduated summa cum laude. He was forty-nine.

Take a look at him the way I know him today. He has a strong and varied vocabulary, at ease among intellectuals and medical technicians. Because of his somewhat leathery complexion and easy swinging gait, he looks for all the world like one of the "good guys" you see in old cowboy shoot-em-up movies on late night television. His voice is a bit harsh now (he was operated on for throat cancer) but his entire demeanor is that of dignity, self-assurance and purpose. He is now known nationwide as an authority on the treatment of the disease of alcoholism. You see him this way, knowing him as I do, and you cannot picture him in the slums of Manila or lying in the Lucky Flophouse.

From 1961 to 1967, he worked as a counselor for the police, for the alcohol-tuberculosis program at the old Firland Sanatorium. During part of that period, 1965 to 1967, he was chief of the Alcoholism Section for the Washington State Department of Health. And in 1967, when they put in the now-famous Cedar Hills Alcoholism Treatment Center, they turned to Ron Fagan, a man whose arrests for drunkenness and vagrancy once ran off the bottom of the charts. He helped design it and he was its founder-director. The "they" who turned to him were former county commissioners Ed Munro, Scott Wallace and John Spellman. Spellman, of course, became county executive when the new county charter went into effect, and it was Spellman and former sheriff Jack Porter, who called on Fagan when Cedar Hills was first discussed. In a large, functional sense, Cedar Hills was Ron Fagan's creation.

Now, sitting in his small, spare office in the Millionair Club, he remembers that sheriff Porter told him, "Ron, you're going to have to learn how to apply for federal grants." "I'll do it my own way, or you'll get another man," Fagan replied. "I apply for federal money and I'll be up to my ears in paperwork. No, this one I do my own way." And Ron Fagan laid down his own special conditions for running Cedar Hills. One was selection of staff and counselors. Almost to a man they were Fagan's own kind, what he calls "former alkies," who had been given special training. "We talked each other's language," he laughs. He fought off the strictures of bureaucracy that might inhibit his program. He conferred closely with such experts in alcoholism treatment as Dr. James Milam, founder of Alcenas, a private treatment center near Kirkland. Ron Fagan's own education never slowed.

In his years with the police department he treated and counseled twelve thousand confirmed alcoholics. These were the habitual drinkers picked up off the street. At Cedar Hills he worked with about twenty-five hundred of the same kind. Follow-up studies of Cedar Hills, conducted by disinterested researchers, showed an astonishing recovery rate of 50 percent. The figure is astonishing because most of Cedar Hills' "student body" were not social drinkers gone wrong; they were hard-core, indigent alcoholics.

At Cedar Hills he initiated a novel technique—the use of video tape. Most of his "clients" came to Ron Fagan with their own, built-in, self-deceptive pictures of themselves. They were quick to be defensive and hostile to suggestions they might even have a problem, and because of the nature of the disease, they were past masters at bluff and deception. Fagan, knowing every nuance of the "alkie language," would video tape their initial interviews with him when they first arrived at Cedar Hills. The interviews were always low-key, friendly, and nonjudgmental. Ron Fagan wrote the book on boozing; he had been one of them, and he knew their world better than they did.

At the end of thirty days of treatment—good diet, reading, lectures, counseling from the master and his "specially trained" former alkies—Fagan would show them the original video tape on their "graduation." A gasping reaction was not uncommon: "My God, was I really *that* bad?"

He followed another precept, formed by Dr. Milam and a few others—namely, that alcoholism is a "primary" disease, not a spinoff from psychological warping or from any other disturbance. For some reason, never fully and scientifically explained, certain drinkers (maybe one in ten, maybe more) cannot drink without becoming alcoholics. "So you have to take the guilt out of it," Fagan has said. "It is just as absurd to point the finger of guilt at an alcoholic as it is to lay personal blame on somebody who has diabetes or cancer. Done right, you can soon find the real man behind the alcohol."

When Ron Fagan retired from Cedar Hills, they gave him a bronze key to the county jail. "Because more than any man, Ron Fagan kept the jails empty during rehabilitation," said one official. Ron Fagan went right on working, giving lectures, counseling and helping young graduate students interested in the field of alcoholism. "I remember once that Spellman warned me," he says. "He said, 'Remember, you'll be doing two hours of work for every hour you volunteer.'"

So this one-time skid road bum went on working. He

worked closely with Dr. Lawrence Bergner, head of the Division of Alcoholism Services of the King County Health Department. He has acted as consultant to the National Institute of Alcohol and Drugs and the Alcohol Institute at the University of Washington. More and more, graduate students were sent to him from all over the United States for advice and instruction. In 1976 he received the Alice Ralls Award from the King County Bar Association, and in 1978 he received the Gold Key Award from the National Council on Alcoholism.

"Orange Blossom." How long ago? My friend Ron Fagan is seventy now. You can find him any morning at the Millionair Club, where he wears the somewhat nebulous title of "Program Planning Advisor." Behind his desk is a sign that lists conditions for help at the Club, one of which is this: "The 'hiding of problem' often hinders us in helping our clients. We will respect your privacy at all times. If you wish to play games . . . GO Elsewhere."

The Millionair Club works with all kinds of service agencies, and it is Fagan, capable of spotting an alkie a block away, who steers those who need it into treatment centers.

How many lives has he saved? How many families did he keep together? How many kids were spared the terror of alcoholic parents? And how do you measure the self-respect he restored to thousands of people? Nobody knows. In the lexicon of alcoholic treatment, the word "cured" is never used; "recovering" is more common because "cure" is a lifetime journey. But my friend Ron Fagan will say, if you ask him, that his own credo always has been "that a cured alcoholic is the one you bury sober." Then the wry smile of a man who has known the world. "And that's the way they'll bury me."

9

Dearly Beloved

I don't practice religion a hell of a lot, but I have always wished somebody would come along and prove that reincarnation really works. And if I come back in another life I want to be about what I am now—a friendly sort of goof, who forms strong attachments to certain people. I have always developed these emotional pulls, a devotion to dissimilar people that is almost childlike. A psychiatrist could probably explain this, but a psychiatrist isn't going to. Most of my friends don't have much in common with each other; they are very different—in demeanor, outlook, wealth and conditions of servitude, if any. They were and are important to me as friends, but more than that, they have given the city fabric and color and sometimes warmth. When I form these attachments, there is an inevitable urge to write about those who count in my life. In some cases I have done so, but finding a reason, the "peg" for a story, has always been the big hang-up. Sadly, I wrote about some of them only after they died. Their death was the "peg" that was needed.

Ever since I got into the writing racket, I've been plagued by that one necessity: to find a "reason" for writing about people. Inevitably, I wrote a lot of stuff about people I didn't care much for, was bored by, or didn't even respect much. I wrote about them because they were momentarily interesting; they had broken an existing record, or done something with a baseball or a football or a hydroplane that got them into the news. When that happened, you got what Red Smith used to call a "plinth," a base on which to build columns; you had a "reason" for writing. The columnist's prayer: Our Father, who art in Heaven, give us this day our daily plinth.

In my lifetime I probably have written thirty or more national magazine stories and maybe six thousand columns for newspapers. If you want to say, "That is too many," go ahead; I agree. You may contend this stuff was lousy, but I say it was just a lot of work. The hardest part, always, was to come up with a suitable reason for writing about someone, to find the editorial "peg" for flipping off a thousand or more words to earn the daily ration of bran mash they paid me.

"Someday I'm going to write a book," I kept saying, mostly to myself. "It will be a book about people I know, people I care for, people who matter, who affected my life or some other lives around them." This book, I swore, would be about people who made a difference to me, who made a difference in the city I love, because of the fact that they existed. No other reasons needed, none given. When the idea of this book first got off the ground (after years of procrastination) I told an editor the names of some people I wanted to get in it. "What is their reason for being in the book?" I was asked.

"You can't just throw some people in a book without a reason for writing about them." Back to square one.

Then one day I had lunch with my friend, Bill Dwyer. Bill is the kind of person I described above, someone you are drawn to for qualities that don't make good news copy, but who, by the mere fact of being alive, gives substance to your life. Bill Dwyer is the kind of attorney that a gunnysack full of graduates from Harvard Law can never hope to be. Not many people know—or remember, if they ever did know—that if it weren't for Bill Dwyer, the Kingdome might have cost the taxpayers much more than it did. In a lawsuit against the original contractors, who had pulled out of the job, he enriched King County by the sum of $12.3 million. In still another suit on behalf of the taxpayers, he insured that Seattle would have major league baseball as the Kingdome's prime tenant. In this landmark case against professional baseball—specifically the American League—he forced the various yahoos who make up the league's ownership to stop jumping around from city to city like a bunch of carnival sharpies scooping up loose change.

When the old Seattle Pilots, circa 1969, were unceremoniously pulled out of Seattle and given to Milwaukee, Bill Dwyer was offended. It offended many other people as well. So Bill set to work, and five years later he forced the American League to create a new franchise and put it in Seattle. For casual baseball fans who wonder why the American League has fourteen franchises and the National League only twelve, this is because of Bill Dwyer. That is, by winning this lawsuit on behalf of King County, he forced the addition not only of the local team, but another one in the city of Toronto, in order to balance the league with an even number of cities holding franchises.

I spent a joyful two weeks in an Everett courtroom watching Bill Dwyer call on baseball tycoon after baseball tycoon, ripping their testimony apart, prevailing over their arrogance with his gentle, deadly cross-examination. When it became clear to the league and its owners that they would all go down the tube with heavy, humiliating civil damages, they hollered "uncle" and Bill settled with them. The terms were simple: the American League would put a new baseball franchise in Seattle—later to become the Mariners—and this franchise, or team, would be locked into a virtually unbreakable lease arrangement that would protect King County taxpayers from any more such piratical pullouts. When the new owners (who got a sweetheart deal from an American League dying to get Bill Dwyer off its back) began to put their team together, I suggested calling it the Seattle Litigants. Like most of my crusades, this one got a big yawn so I temporarily retired from the crusading industry.

Anyway, when a settlement ended the trial, newspapermen polled the jurors to see how they would have voted if the case had actually gone to the jury room. The projected score was clearly in favor of King County and Bill Dwyer. One woman juror said that when Dwyer brought the rich tycoons into the dock for testimony, "I tried not to be impressed by their fancy suits, so I imagined them without any clothes on." This so delighted Bill that when he bought his opening day tickets to the Mariners' first game in the Kingdome in April 1976 he gave them to the woman juror and stayed home himself.

Bill has won a lot of other cases, too. He has brought in huge anti-trust judgments on behalf of farmers, loggers, orchardists and theater owners who were getting the shaft from unfair competition or monopoly price-fixing.

Throughout his career, Bill Dwyer has never cooled in his strong affection for the First Amendment. Early in life, Bill developed the belief that free expression, in all its forms, wasn't the worst idea our founding fathers ever concocted; he does not believe that it is healthy to have a bunch of fundamentalist nitwits and other retarded clock-stoppers telling everybody what films they should see, what books they should read, or what art objects they can view. He has handled several of these so-called "cause" cases for no fee at all. In these matters, and a few others, Bill Dwyer and I have common beliefs. Not the least of the beliefs we share is a devotion to the memory of Charlie Burdell.

I told Bill I wanted to write some stuff about Charlie Burdell. "The problem," I said, "is that some of my literary advisers think I've got to have a reason for writing about Charlie. Frankly, I'm stuck. After all, Charlie's been dead and gone for some years now, and they don't think he would fit into the theme of a book. You got any ideas on that?"

Bill's reply was instantaneous. He has a way of shoveling aside the non-essentials and getting to the heart of a matter. "You should write about Charlie Burdell because he was a wonderful guy. You should write about him because he was a great lawyer and a good friend. You should let people know that he was an important, decent guy to have around." That cleared up my thinking about the need to have a reason for writing about Charlie Burdell.

One fine March evening in 1957, an airplane bearing the prestigious personage of James Duff, a former senator from Pennsylvania, arrived at Seattle–Tacoma International Airport. His arrival did not go unreported. Ex-Senator Duff was an important figure in a big story of that time. He was known as Dave Beck's "personal legal counsel" when Beck faced the inquisitors of what was then known as the McClellan Rackets Committee. The Teamster leader was hauled in before the committee and invoked the Fifth Amendment dozens of times, each time saying it was "on the advice of my counsel, former Senator Duff."

The events of that summer forcefully shaped U.S. politics for years to come. A handsome young member of the Mc-Clellan Committee would later become president of the United States. His brother, Robert F. Kennedy, the committee's chief counsel, would become U.S. attorney general. For Beck, who eventually went to prison in the summer of 1962, it was five long years of litigation. Rarely, if ever, has a powerful figure been required to defend himself in so many cases at the same time.

Beck was indicted by the federal government on charges that he evaded personal income taxes and filed false information returns for the Teamsters Union in 1950. He was indicted in the state of Washington for embezzling $1,900 from the sale of a union car. The federal indictments charged him with evading taxes in the years 1951 to 1953, and for causing false information to be filed for the union in 1951 and 1952. He was also indicted on charges of violating the Taft-Hartley Act.

In all, Dave Beck answered to twelve counts and four indictments. By any measurement, considering the federal and state resources allied against him, considering the state of public opinion and the legal talent out to convict him, Beck was in deep trouble. But in the end he was convicted on only three counts—embezzlement of $1,900 from sale of the union car, and two counts of filing false information on behalf of his union.

The appearance here of ex-Senator James Duff remained

somewhat a mystery for a long time. But when I asked Charlie Burdell about that visit, he supplied at least part of the answer. "I guess," he said, "that Dave sent for Senator Duff to come out here and look me over."

It was Charlie Burdell, a Seattle attorney, who almost pulled off a legal miracle on behalf of his client. He defended Beck through three trials, four appeals and numerous appellant arguments. Three times Burdell took Beck's $1,900 embezzlement case to the State Supreme Court, which split each time, 4–4, over whether the conviction should be upheld. And only later did the United States Supreme Court itself, in a 4–3 decision, finally uphold Beck's conviction.

It was during those years, and because of my friendship with Bill Dwyer, that I got to know Charlie Burdell. Like most of us, I'm a sucker for stereotypes, so in reading accounts of the Beck case in newspapers and magazines, I formed a picture of Burdell: he would be dapper, dashing, handsome and witty. He would wear tailored suits and he would need a social secretary to fend off invitations to cocktail parties and fancy dinners. He would use meticulous English and he would dazzle people with his courtroom tactics. He would be, as I imagined him, a cross between Louis Nizer and Edward Bennett Williams, with maybe a touch of Houdini in his make-up.

Then I met Charlie. I remember thinking, "This guy couldn't get a walk-on part in a Perry Mason show." Charlie was short, a bit overweight, and he looked for all the world like some dumpy third-string catcher called in to pinch-hit when the game was lost. His coat was usually open, his tie loosened, and he often wore his glasses pulled back to rest on the top of his head. When I mentioned how surprised I was when I first met Charlie, a friend who knew him well said,

"Yeah, Charlie is the only guy I know who could walk out of Littler's wearing a three hundred dollar suit and get picked up for vagrancy three blocks away." As I got to know Charlie better, I found that conversation with him could be distracting. When we drank coffee together he would stir his with a ball-point pen. Quite often his shirttail would be out. His language, I found, was beautifully explicit in a courtroom, but in private he sounded something like a fight manager. He often referred to a client as "my guy," and he could dismiss a whole case with, "Yeah, I was lucky. I got my guy out of that one. I guess he was innocent."

"I did lousy at Bowdoin," he said one time, referring to the college he had attended in Maine. "But Bowdoin was a good outfit." How many people have you met who would refer to a distinguished seat of learning as an "outfit?" He had earlier gone to Colgate on an athletic scholarship (the bull pen catcher analogy, I found out, was quite apt). He quit after one year at Colgate because the football coach wouldn't let him turn out for baseball. Later he went to Nebraska where he got his law degree in 1939. "They didn't exactly kick me out of Bowdoin," he told me, "but they suggested maybe I oughta knock off for a year and go to work."

After law school, Charlie got a job in the anti-trust division of the U.S. Justice Dept. There he became friends with Tom Clark, later the U.S. attorney general. Because of his friendship with Clark, Burdell wound up on the staff of Justice Robert Jackson, chief U.S. prosecutor in the Nuremberg trials. Charlie helped prosecute Herman Goering and Rudolph Hess and a few other delinquents who gave us full employment back in the forties. I used to pump Charlie for lore about the Nazis, but he had a way of deflecting you by saying, "That wasn't much, but wait'll I tell you about that German general I got to know, a helluva guy."

He drank coffee, a lot of coffee, having given up booze years before I got to know him. We used to say that Charlie was "lint prone." He also used to spill ashes all over those three hundred dollar Littler suits. And when you were with Charlie, the clock never seemed to matter. The ultimate expression of friendship from this incredibly busy and successful lawyer was making you feel that when he talked to you it was the most important thing he would do all day. When he discussed a case, the story was usually spliced with anecdotes about how he misjudged a juror, or the way an opposing attorney scored against him, or how he stumbled on a good point by accident. He had a strong ego, but it was balanced by a genuine humility. "What's this I hear about you naming your kid after me?" he demanded of a young lawyer. "That's right, Charlie, he's named after you—you and John Stuart Mill." "That's okay, I guess," Charlie said. "But I just want you to know how much that means to a boob like me."

His relaxed, almost diffident behavior at a hearing, a trial, or in deposition, was profoundly deceptive. His easy manner made him a hero to some of the younger lawyers, and a few tried to imitate him. "They couldn't do it," an older lawyer told me. "What they didn't know was that Charlie stayed up till midnight getting ready. He was mulling the case over while he watched some jackass TV show. Besides, he had more law in his head than they had in their libraries."

There was one instance when Charlie made a big impression at a hearing. Where most lawyers would be carrying a brief case full of papers, notes and reminders, Charlie arrived with a single book. While the hearing proceeded, Charlie sat at his table, seemingly engrossed in his reading. Soon the attention of everyone in the room was drawn to Charlie's seeming preoccupation with his book. He would make an occasional appropriate remark, perhaps an objection, and go on reading.

The entire procedure swung his way, and it was only later that another attorney, his curiosity now feverish, maneuvered himself to look over Charlie's shoulder at the book. Its title was *Guide to Model Railroading*.

He ranked as tops among a small corps of lawyers who would not duck tough cases, which is why he was never impressed by won-lost records, no matter how famous the attorney. He knew what ball parks they played in. Charlie took on a multitude of tough criminal and civil cases, involving anti-trust and tax fraud—the Hans Forster tax fraud suit, Moore vs. Standard Oil, Chelan PUD vs. General Electric, the City of San Francisco vs. Allis Chalmers. There is a penalty for taking on such cases and Burdell paid it. He was afflicted by insomnia; he replayed cases in his mind, and because he saw good in almost everyone, he fretted over the welfare of even the least deserving of his clients. He made no real distinctions—at least outwardly—in what the rest of us, thinking in absolutes, would classify as good and bad. "There are good guys and there are bad guys," he once said, "and there are guys who are just awful." Because he liked Dave, the Beck defeat hit him hard. One of the town's younger attorneys, who had just lost an affair of the heart, told me of a pact he made with Charlie. "I promised to stop worrying about my ex-girl friend if he would quit worrying about Dave Beck. But I caught him cheating on me."

Charlie Burdell was a man to whom the law was life, a man who cared—deep down, really cared—about his own clients and the rights of human beings. He thought a lot about kids and young lawyers trying to make it, and he didn't like to see people get pushed around. In his late fifties Charlie suffered a series of heart attacks and the last one proved fatal. On what turned out to be the final day of Charlie's life, Bill Dwyer paid another of his daily visits to the hospital room. He found Charlie propped up in bed leafing through some legal documents, happily immersed in the great driving force of his life.

"You shouldn't be doing that," Bill said. "You should think of something else. Why don't you think about the Peloponnesian War?"

"Yeah, maybe you're right," Charlie said. "As a matter of fact, I've been thinking about Shakespeare lately."

They talked of some of the kings Shakespeare wrote plays about, and then Bill said, "There's some new research coming out about Richard III. It shows that Richard III wasn't as bad a guy as Shakespeare made him out to be." Charlie seemed pleased by this news. "Well, I'm glad they're finally saying something good about him," he said.

A few hours later Charlie died. As the saying goes, they packed the joint at his funeral. They were all there, ordinary friends, former governors, senators, one-time clients, judges and fellow attorneys. Something rich and wonderful was gone, but at the end, Charlie had it better than Richard III. People were saying good things about him all along.

It was through Charlie that I got to know Dave Beck. This was before they clanked the gates behind him at McNeil Island, where he did nearly three years of hard time. Sometimes I would join Beck and Charlie for morning coffee at George's Cafe, a Greek place that got wiped out by the downtown freeway. Even then, only a few weeks away from the sneezer, Dave was busy, wheeling and dealing in real estate, loudly proclaiming his innocence and making plans for the future. He is possibly the most indestructible man I have ever known.

Young people, unfamiliar with Dave Beck, might find it difficult to imagine his power when Dave was at the top of his game. It is scarcely an exaggeration to say that not a wheel rolled in America without Dave's okay. He was first head of the Western Conference of Teamsters, then became president of the International Brotherhood of Teamsters. When he became Teamsters president, he transferred some $8 million of union funds from Indianapolis banks into Seattle banks. Bankers, industrialists, various business leaders and governors sought his counsel or approval. He became president of the University of Washington's Board of Regents. He was a guest of President Eisenhower in the White House, and his proclamations on the national economy were listened to and often made big news.

The day he returned to Seattle from McNeil Island, I went up to his suite in the Olympic Hotel. The place was so full of lawyers, accountants, old friends and Teamsters officials that you could scarcely breathe. It was as though he had never left. He held court, so to speak, striding up and down the room, gesturing, laughing, shouting and berating the federal prison system. When the room thinned out, I talked to him about doing a magazine story that would outline his views on how prisons could be changed and improved. He was excited by the idea and so was I.

A few days later he called me and said, "The goddamned lawyers won't let me do it. I've still got the parole board to think about, and they say I can't do it."

Later he would get a full pardon from President Ford, but by then his prison time was long ago, and a Beck story—that news "peg" again—probably wouldn't sell. He retreated into a three-bedroom apartment on Pill Hill, the Gainsborough, and I would drop in to see him now and then. His name was not listed on the apartment directory and he had an unlisted telephone number. He had gotten into some trouble in McNeil for helping a fellow prisoner who needed money to see his family, and at one point he was thrown into solitary confinement. But he wouldn't bend or break, and he came out the way he went in—roaring defiance.

Of his time in prison, Beck resolutely refused to let anyone believe he had truly been punished. "Prison added eight or ten years to my life," he would say. "When I ran the Teamsters I was working eighteen hours a day and traveling all the time. Hell, I had it a lot tougher in World War I than I ever did at McNeil Island. I lost twenty-two pounds in prison, I exercised a lot, got plenty of sleep, and I got a damned good rest out of it."

Now and then we talked about Charlie Burdell and other lawyers. To Beck, lawyers were not exalted professionals; they were people you hired, the way you hired a doctor or a guy to carry out the garbage. "We beat 'em on everything," he said, speaking of his old tax troubles. "The only thing they convicted me on was a report that went in from the Joint Council of Teamsters. It carried the signature of Frank Brewster and Don McDonald—he was the auditor—and they testified they put it on my desk. It did not carry my signature but technically, I was president, and I was held responsible."

"And I hope to Christ"—Dave's crescendos of bombast are something to behold—"that my mother never sees Heaven if I ever saw that goddamned piece of paper! That's the only thing I went over to the Island on!"

Watergate broke about that time and it became plain that the country was being run by a group of felons. The subject of trials and prison terms for such as Haldeman, Ehrlichman, Mitchell, Colson, Liddy, Hunt, and other malefactors was much in the news. This could set Beck off on another striding, gesturing monologue. "You're not going to accomplish a damned thing by sending people like that to prison. A man like Ehrlichman—mind you, I don't even know the fella. There's no sense to sending a man like that to prison or any of the others. You've gotta find a damned sight better method than prison to be fair to the taxpayer and everybody else. What the hell's the sense in it? There's nothing to be gained by sending Ehrlichman—like I said, I don't even know the fella—to a penitentiary and imposing a tremendous sentence on his wife and children, and the same holds true for the rest of 'em."

I never was quite sure if Dave was arguing the case for Ehrlichman or himself, most probably the latter. But he could really unwind on the topic. He said, "I contend that first offenders on 95 percent of cases should never go to the penitentiary. Give 'em a hell of a fine. Give 'em thirty or sixty days to let 'em see what it's like. Then bring 'em back into society and see if they can behave."

Beck is first of all, before anything else, a businessman. He sees labor as being part of business and he sees labor negotiations the way he sees any other business deal—you bargain in the marketplace for the price of labor the same way you bargain for shipping rates or warehouse rental. I always enjoyed these monologues, and I often wonder what it would have been like to have had this access to him in the days of enormous power—when almost anything he said would, as it sometimes did, shake the town. Beck is about as close to George F. Babbitt, the central figure in Sinclair Lewis' classic novel, as you will find. Most of his friends were (and still are) businessmen, and he was loudly proud of his Elks Lodge membership and assorted civic awards. He got some big citation from the realtors back in the fifties, plus some other trappings that make businessmen feel warm and loved in Babbitland. Probably the one thing that hurt him most during his tumultuous downfall was the way some of these business friends, particularly bankers, placed themselves at a discreet distance from him. They owed a lot to Dave Beck.

And the thing that most rankled him about Watergate is the fact that these white collar break-in artists often went free, before trial and sentencing, on their personal recognizance. After all, wasn't he a guest of the White House once? Wasn't he a certified, flag-saluting, apple-pie patriot, who fought communism all his life? Where did they get off, taking him to McNeil in handcuffs?

"They put me under ninety thousand-dollar bond and that damned thing remained there for damned near five years!" he thundered. "You take 6 percent on ninety thousand, that's fifty-four hundred a year I lost—about four hundred a month! How in the world could I ever have jumped out of the country? They'd have seized everything I owned."

Beck is almost a purist in personal habits. He never has taken a drink, never smoked, and reveres his dead mother, whose name he frequently invokes when he wants to swear to the truth of something. He never uses foul language. He luxuriates in an occasional "goddamn" or "hell," but he would be profoundly offended if someone used more fashionable four-letter words in his presence.

I have often thought that people interested in Seattle's past are missing a bet by not talking to Dave. He has almost total recall on buildings, houses, and neighborhoods of Seattle; he knows a lot about Lake Union development and quite a bit about downtown. He used to talk, sometimes, of his days as a boy when he shot rats for bounty under the old University Bridge to help support his mother. Some years ago I recorded a few things Dave said about Seattle's future development; his foresight is startling when reviewed today. He was then very bullish on the Denny Regrade.

"The only thing that ever held the Regrade back in my opinion—I could be wrong, because I don't have factual data—are the downtown business people. Downtown held it back because it was opposed to residential development on the Regrade. For a long time you couldn't build a high rise apartment there. When we built the Grosvenor House—there were about ten of us behind it—it was the first high-rise ever built out there. We didn't have much trouble because of the tremendous demand for housing after World War II.

"But now I think over the next ten or fifteen or twenty years, you're going to find almost a duplicate of the apartment construction they had in Vancouver. Because it's those people, the people living in those Regrade apartments, that are going to have to feed the retail downtown area, or that area's going to continually slide away. I may not see it, but future generations will see that Fifth and Denny, or right around there, will be the center of Seattle. I think there'll be a tremendous residential development from First Avenue clear across the Regrade to Eastlake and Westlake. From the shores of Lake Union up to Denny Way will be mostly commercial. But from Pine Street north to Mercer Street, you'll see solid apartment houses, because there's no view like that in the world."

Looking over the Regrade today, with condos hopscotching across the landscape, the old lion hit rather close to what's happening. Dave and I got to be pretty good friends over the years. If somebody got through to him to request an interview, he'd sometimes call me "just to check the fella out." If a story intrigued him in the paper, he would call to expound his views on it. About four years ago, when the newspaper guild took a strike vote during negotiations with the *P–I*, he called several times "to see how things are goin'." He was, after all, and he never let you forget it, the man who put the muscle of the Teamsters behind the guild when it struck the *P–I* in 1936. "You gotta have a strike vote," he said, at one point. "That shows you mean business. But you tell those fellas in the guild that a strike isn't what you want. What you want are wages, hours and conditions, and you gotta have the other unions behind you in this."

Last spring there came another of Dave's cheerful calls. "I just wanted to tell you June 16 is coming up. That's my birthday. I'll be eighty-eight, by God, and I'll outlive the lot of you."

Dave may be right; we shall see.

What is not in doubt is that Dave is profoundly different from a woman I once knew and cared for. It is difficult to imagine Beck, or even Charlie Burdell, residing on the same planet with Betty Bowen. I sometimes wondered if I did.

She used to come winging down Fifth Ave. in her white 1955 Jaguar XK140 on her way to meet some benighted poet or perhaps an artist who needed to have his paintings moved someplace. Or maybe she would stop at Trader Vic's where she "did publicity," sweeping grandly into the room where she would hold court at a favorite table, her ivory cigarette holder tilted in the air, clapping her hands for service and emitting great harpie-like guffaws, as she spoofed the Tallulah Bankhead role she was playing. She was a little more like Auntie Mame, really, and I sometimes called her "Mary Worth" because of her obsession to make the world perfect. She knew, of course, that the world could never be perfect, but she awakened every morning with a determination to see that her part of that world would be better than it was the night before.

By the sheer force of her being and the ever-changing constellation of her personality, she was a Seattle celebrity. Charlie Michener, managing editor of the old *Seattle* magazine, called one time. He said they were doing a story on Betty Bowen and could I tell him, was Betty Bowen really important? "We know about how she helps artists and calls people and how witty she is," Charlie said, "but is she really important to Seattle?" He had me on that one. I have pondered that question for some years; my answer, I suppose, is longer than it needs to be.

A city to be a good city requires some kind of adhesive. It needs creative people to hold it together, to give it continuity, substance and character. Seattle is blessed to have had a lot of such people—catalysts, if you will—whose imagination and force made good things happen in the city. It was Anna Clise, be it remembered, who in 1909 led the founding of Children's Orthopedic Hospital, which is now a monument to the city's style and humanity. It was Jess Epstein, who fought off the developers and real estate honchos to create Yesler Terrace, a model for low-income housing. It was Jim Ellis, who gave up years of his time and energy to rally a consensus that cleaned up our waters, expanded our parks and funded the Kingdome. More than any one man, Victor Steinbrueck, the maverick architect, pulled the city together and saved the Pike Place Market.

In her own time and in her own way, Betty Bowen was one of these catalysts. While her genius did not create buildings and parks, physical entities you can point to and measure, she helped give us direction, a sense of place, a feeling for dignity and beauty, a respect for small things and small people, and a decent regard for our past. Was she important? Betty Bowen was like a small pebble dropped in a large pond of quiet water; she radiated ripples and waves that resulted in opinions and actions, and she worked in strange ways her wonders to perform.

"Emil?" The voice could be plaintive on the telephone. She always called me "Emil"—God knows why—and she could be alternately plaintive and childlike, or loud with indignation and outrage. "Emil, there is an old building down in the Regrade and they're going to tear it down. You must do something about that. You must stop consorting with your low friends in bars and do something decent for a change." There would follow the instant "click" of the receiver. "I don't know of anyone with a greater facility for saying good-bye by simply hanging up," the late Irving Clark once said of her.

She would randomly call and say accusingly, "Emil, you haven't done anything to help the bear lately." Early on I would sputter, "What bear, for Pete's sake?" I learned later that for her, at least, the bear was a symbol; the bear was endangered, therefore all living things, all good things, are endangered. Save an old building and you have "helped the bear." Write something nice about the Audubon Society and the bear, at least momentarily, was protected.

Betty Bowen moved in a surprisingly narrow circle. Because she was vibrant, warm, and often hilariously funny, she was much in social demand, but she led a possessively private life. She did her daily duties, nurturing good press notices for Trader Vic's and the Seattle Art Museum, where she also worked part-time. She devoted enormous energy to such pursuits as getting an unread writer together with a publisher, seeing to it that a gallery had a showing for a young artist, or exhorting editors and writers to take notice of "the really important things." Her private friends were often the wealthy, the likes of Kayla and Ned Skinner and Anne Hauberg, and because she exhorted these people, good things happened. When he got to know her better—this was after he called me—Charlie Michener concluded: "More than anyone in town, she provides a catalyst between different segments of the community. And in the world of the arts, she is a mother, aunt and broker, all wrapped into one."

She despised all monstrous things, be they freeways, buildings or bombast; all giant schemes and unshapely developments. She once marched up to a big shopping center developer, waving her ivory cigarette holder, and declared: "I pray for you every day—in a *landmark* church!"

When a pitiful band of protesters marched against the scarring, brutal downtown freeway in Seattle, Betty Bowen was too ill to march. But she hired a surrogate from the Millionair Club who marched in her place, carrying her sign: "I am divided about sin but against cement."

When I asked her once what was the best thing we might do to improve Seattle, she snapped: "Put it back!"

When Betty was a young girl, she met Morris Graves for the first time and ran home and said, "Mother, I've just met a starving artist. Bake some cookies!"

"She opened doors for us," said the artist Leo Kenney one time. "She was the runner between our garrets and Hunts Point and Broadmoor. She had magic powers."

Betty did the hard things for those she believed in. She hauled paintings for artists, setting up their shows, giving them food and money to subsist. The portraitist, Jan Thompson, remembers that "back in the late forties when we were all starving, she would leave boxes of goodies on our doorsteps." She helped Morris Graves and she helped Mark Tobey and she helped Leo Kenney and Richard Gilkey long before they became widely known and celebrated.

Once I ran into her at lunch. She was sitting with a sallow-faced young man, who seemed inordinately shy and ill at ease in Trader Vic's. "Emil, this is Richard," she said. "Richard is an extraordinarily talented poet who will become very famous someday." Then, turning to "Richard" she waved her cigarette holder at me and continued: "Richard, this is Emil. He is a wretch, a perfectly horrid wretch sometimes, and I often think he has the taste of a billygoat. But Emil is going to help you, aren't you, Emil? Emil is going to write something nice about you and let everybody know how good you are." Then back to me, "If you don't do as I say, I will set the bear on you."

The raccoons in her neighborhood were hungry and Betty would dash to her Queen Anne home to put raw eggs in a bowl for the raccoons. She wrote furious letters about people who spread pesticides. She kept a sharp, skeptical eye on all doings of the Humane Society. She is the only person in Seattle I ever met who belonged to the American Society for the Preservation of the Burro. Her written messages were baroque, sometimes containing unfathomable references, and they were always signed with a small circle, two little eye dots, and a moonish smile. That I didn't save her notes is only one of the penalties one pays for leading a disorderly life. But I take the liberty here of reprinting a Christmas message, first preserved by Charlie Michener in *Seattle* magazine, and written to her close friends, Kayla and Ned Skinner:

"It has become my mission during these twelve interminable days of Christmas (ever has the populace been gulled by the sop of holidays—panem et circensus—how it wearies me) to deliver to you, with suitable blandishments, a message of warmth, affection and any number of desperately plebian hugs and kisses, the delivery of which I fear may prove inadequate, the rigid code of my upbringing having disallowed effusion and gaucheries of every kind.''

The letter epitomizes the Betty Bowen I knew. She was put off by the big, organized religions, and since Christmas is always an horrendous, commercial blast, it saddened her that we have somehow lost our way in celebrating the birth of Christ. She could shed tears—I have seen her burst into weeping at the sight of a derelict—but her sentiment always was carefully rationed, lest the bad drive out the good, an emotional Gresham's Law that would dilute the genuine. Her "rigid code of my upbringing" did more than "disallow effusion and gaucheries"; it disallowed tolerance of the shoddy, the banal, the false and the base. When confronted by blatant hypocrisy or selfishness her wit could slash like a razor's edge. Once, to an editor she did not respect, she left an April 1 message: "April, Fool."

When I first met Betty Bowen she was a patient in the old Firlands Sanitarium with suspected tuberculosis. She was, then, a beautiful girl with long dark hair, and as visitors streamed in and out it became apparent that they were coming to be encouraged and entertained by her, not she by them. This was in 1951.

She was always attractive to men. When an aging roue fondled her knee under the table at a dinner party, she looked him in the face and cooled his ardor in a loud voice, "Do you realize there are only three hundred grizzly bears left in the northern hemisphere?" Nothing dazzled her, certainly not the phony art crowd of New York in which she found herself at a cocktail party in someone's penthouse. This being that kind of gathering, lights were dimmed after a few drinks, and shadowy pairings took place. To her instant disgust, Betty found a man nuzzling her closely in the dimness, and abruptly the room was detonated by a glass-shattering voice that literally rose out of the Skagit Flats where she was raised. "Get your tongue out of my eustachian tube!" One draws a veil.

"What have you done for the bear lately?" It seems so long ago. Do better, be better, write more honestly; the bear is endangered; values are endangered; so are people, beauty, integrity, all good things that should be preserved. She was not especially impressed by the alleged wonders of organized medicine. She thought of dentists as less skilled than a reasonably competent carpenter. She despised formal pomposity of all kinds.

News of her terminal illness spread as a shock wave among those who knew and loved her. When the gravity of her condition was apparent, when the doctors prepared to operate on her for a brain tumor, she called out to her husband John, "Can't they let the knife slip?" The knife did not slip, but in a short time this woman who would not live life by half got her wish. A few days later she died quietly at home in the night. When family members and close friends examined her estate, they were astounded to learn that her art collection alone was appraised at more than $200,000. These paintings were gifts of love and gratitude from the many artists she had helped in her lifetime—Tobey, Graves, Callahan, Gilkey and so many others.

One afternoon a few days after her memorial services, John Bowen picked me up and we drove to their house on Queen Anne, a few blocks below the point that is now known as Betty Bowen Park.

John disappeared into another room for a minute, then returned to hand me a figure wrapped in tissue. "Betty always wanted you to have this," he said. It was a small ivory carving of a polar bear.

I never knew Betty Bowen in college but I'm sure, with her own high standards of taste and learning, she might have considered me as little more than a jock pushing his luck. She would have had a point. The University of Washington campus scared hell out of me the first time I saw it. There were all these people signing up for classes, seeming to know each other, being confident of what they were up to. Just the spaciousness of the campus terrified me. When I got my class schedule, I made notes to find out which building was which and actually walked the distances, building to building, to be sure I could make it in the ten minutes they allowed between classes. I was in on probation with a grade point average that resembled a pitcher's lifetime batting record. In short, I was in on a pass—one flunk and out—and for the first time in my life I was scared into working hard.

By underlining, rereading and sometimes memorizing, I finally put together what I never had before—study habits. I spent long hours in the library, or if it was spring, sitting on the grass in front of Denny Hall, trying to dig Shakespeare and learning about the Law of Diminishing Returns in Econ I. At noon, I ate lousy lunches in the old Commons where they taught "home economics" majors how to fry bananas. A few of the profs ate there, and I shamelessly sat myself down at their tables, trying to soak up what I could from their casual conversations.

In this way I met an associate professor named Mel Jacobs, who taught anthropology, and he so caught me up with his amiable erudition that I signed on quickly for his class. In this way, too, I met another anthropologist, Viola Garfield, and sociologist Elton Guthrie, whose classes I also took. That first year I signed up for introductory French, because among my multiple deficiencies in high school, I needed a foreign language. But after a couple of weeks I got out of that French class fast because I was in over my head; one failing grade and I'd be out on a very skimpy job market. During this time I also met an associate professor with the melodious name of Garland Ethel.

I took English poetry from Gar Ethel. He taught with a strong, eloquent intensity, bringing to life the works of Shelley, Keats, Byron and Wordsworth. Because I hung around his office a lot and seemed to take an interest in what he was teaching, Gar Ethel came to like me. In my sopho-more year I had to go into the hospital for a radical mastoid operation, and I lay up at Swedish for three weeks with my head bound up like an Egyptian mummy. Gar Ethel used to take the bus from the University District up to Swedish Hos-pital, a miserable trip in the dark of winter. He brought books, and he would sit by my bed and read aloud to me, hunched up close to my half-good ear that wasn't covered with bandages. We developed a friendship that lasted through many years.

Because he was almost monk-like in his devotion to making things right in the world, he was branded a radical by the panic-driven dullards of the McCarthy era. He got hauled up before the Canwell Committee, a state legislative group run by a dreary apostle of reaction in that period, and Gar Ethel's name and picture were splashed all over the papers as some kind of enemy of America.

Was he a communist? How the hell should I know? If we ever discussed communism, I've forgotten what was said. Mostly we talked of poetry and literature and the decent things to be found in mankind. Garland Ethel was no more an enemy of America than Shirley Temple was. He was a good, decent, compassionate man, who had the kind of love for humanity that you will rarely find anywhere, and this includes a hell of a lot of pulpits.

How tragic the end. In mid-September two years ago, Gar Ethel inexplicably shot and killed his wife, the lovely Clarissa, who worked so many years in the University Bookstore, along with Clarissa's sister and brother-in-law. Then he turned the gun on himself and died five days later in a hospital. In my desk at the time was a warm personal letter saying in part, "See here, Watkins, the years must not advance as they do without our seeing more of each other. Call me and we will set a date for dinner." I didn't call and I am sorry.

What conditions of emotion, frustration and advancing age resulted in such a tragedy are beyond anyone's speculation. His final act was not the man at all. At a small memorial service, Dick Carbray seemed to express the concern of all of us who loved Gar Ethel: "What a crowning unfairness it would be if his life were assessed and defined in terms of those tragic seconds and minutes in Laurelhurst, rather than in terms of the forty-two years he gave to the university."

Because of my dread of flunking out of college, I actually did master the knack of good study habits. My high school record, riddled with deficiencies, gave little hope of obtaining a degree, but I picked up a few As and Bs along the way and they let me stay in. And because of hanging out in the Commons, getting to know the profs and instructors, I ended up taking a wide variety of courses. I got what you might call a smorgasbord of an education; the university, for me, turned into one big feast, a buffet at which I sampled and tasted only those things I liked. My formal education may have had no focus, no purpose, no goal. But it was a lot of fun.

On some days, if I wasn't pressured, I'd casually drop into a new class, one I didn't belong in, just to taste another sample. Nobody seemed to object. So one afternoon, I dropped in on a history class, taught by a guy I'd heard about, but never seen.

He came into the room, carrying a few notes on index cards, a small man, with delicate features, and a full rich head of hair turning only slightly gray at the temples. He half bowed to the class, in a courtly, deferential manner, and then he began talking. He said he would like to apologize for this particular lecture because he hadn't really done the necessary research on the naval battle he was about to discuss. The course was Modern English History, and suddenly he launched into a dissertation on the Battle of Jutland that kept me utterly enthralled for fifty minutes.

It was his voice, a voice with intonations that made dry material seem interesting, and interesting stuff inspiring. I would come to know that voice well, learn what it could do to people in years to come. But this day, in a soft, unpretentious British accent with nuances and subtleties that drove his points home, he talked about the Battle of Jutland. As he rolled on, you began to visualize the ships in the North Sea, the fog and the wind and the rain. Referring but occasionally to his notes, he gave tonnages, strategy, gun emplacements, types of guns, strengths and weaknesses of the commanders, putting the battle into perspective as it pertained to English sea power.

I guess some people were affected that way when they first heard Olivier doing Shakespeare. All I remember is that I went out of the professor's class, somewhat dazed by his eloquence, and determined that I would take this man's courses, get to know him, perhaps well enough to sit with him at his leisure.

That was the first time I ever saw Giovanni Costigan.

Eventually, I took ten hours from Costigan on Modern English History. But that is not important. What emerged in the years to come was an increasing awareness of the importance of this diminutive figure of a man who committed himself to a life of deep involvement, of passionate, outspoken concern about contemporary problems. His small stature, his gentle, courtly demeanor, are deceiving. He has the instincts of a gamecock, and his ability to probe, project, stimulate, explore, debate and, yes, inflame, set him apart. When liberalism sort of went on the skids during the radicalism of the sixties, a radicalism that hardened conservative reaction on the right, he remained openly, proudly liberal. Conservatives always knew their man.

During many of those years the name of Giovanni Costigan shook the crockery in the Rainier Club and tightened knuckles of the old crocks in it. To the best of my knowledge, no figure in university history, and that would include Henry Suzzallo, J. Allen Smith and Vernon Louis Parrington, was so controversial. This is because Giovanni, like few others in academia, had the courage to take his views off campus and into public arenas of debate. Efforts to get him fired were common. Because of his outspoken liberalism he was branded a communist; some called him a "tool of Moscow," or a "Red rat." I got to know him better during these years, and once, when he denounced the shoddy nature of a scare film called *Communism On The Map*, the abuse reached another crescendo. I went out to see him in his small, cluttered office in Smith Hall, and he remarked, with a faint, wry smile: "In the beginning I was only trying to stimulate discussion of the film. But later, when I heard the click of the revolver over the telephone, I realized the discussion had moved to another area."

He began to get abusive phone calls at 3:00 A.M. "But I will not shut off my phone," he said, resolutely. "I will not give them the satisfaction." As hate campaigns always are, this one was organized. Mail came to him from distant points in the country from people who could not conceivably have heard of him. But Giovanni, ever the courtly respecter of debate, answered each letter in his careful, tiny handwriting.

"It is not a pleasant thing, being hated," he told me once. This time I had dropped by his home near the campus, where he lives with his wife Amne. "You don't hate anyone," he said. "You hold no hatred for any man. But it's awful to realize that there are people out there"—he gestured toward the window—"people unknown to you, who would destroy you if they could. It is very distressing," he added with the trace of a smile, "especially when one is so inoffensive."

By no means is he inoffensive. He debated the right wing's favorite superstar, William F. Buckley, and took his measure before ten thousand people in Hec Edmondson Pavilion. Even Giovanni's admirers were startled (Buckley certainly was) when Costigan, using the classic European method in debating, opened with a savage attack on much of what Buckley had written and what he stood for. Buckley never quite recovered; the urbane easterner lowered the level of the debate by using such words as "crap" in his attempts to refute Giovanni's points, and lost his temper when the debate ended.

For a while in the fifties, even as the sewage of the McCarthy era gradually dissipated, Costigan's name rarely was mentioned in local papers. At least one radio station had a standing rule, summed up in the edict, one newscaster told me, "Never mention that bastard's name on the air." So much for the First Amendment. When I wanted to do a story on Costigan, arguing that he would make fascinating reading, certainly worthy of some understanding comment, it was suggested that any favorable story on Costigan would not be greeted with joy at the *P–I*. But in the mid-sixties, I decided to do the story anyway, and I learned a lot about my one-time teacher.

I interviewed several university administrative and faculty people and found that many shared a strong unanimity of opinion on his virtues. Solomon Katz, then the university provost, was quite eager to get on the record. "You may count me among his warmest admirers," he said. "I have been a Giovanni fan for years." Among his colleagues, he was known for his unfailing courtesy, his sensitivity to the problems of others, and his interest in the progress of younger members of the faculty. I was told that he had once delivered a paper before a group of historians in Canada, an incident which reminded me of that long ago day when I bootlegged my way into his classroom. When he finished his paper, a visiting scholar rose in tribute and said: "This is the first time I have ever heard such a paper read aloud and emerge as poetry."

He is more than a mere poker into history; he is a man of poetry, of literature, of politics; a man of grace and erudition. For a long time, the university's shining literary star was Theodore Roethke, the Pulitzer Prize-winning poet. As it happened, Roethke became ill and was unable to teach for a protracted period. It was the English department which turned to Costigan, of the history department, to conduct Roethke's classes in poetry.

He publishes very little, this man with such facility in our language. As a specialist in English history, his book *Makers of Modern England* was published by MacMillan. He also published a biography of Freud. Perhaps his best-known work is his *History of Modern Ireland*. But essentially, Costigan has been content as a scholar and a teacher, superb on both counts, and a catalyst in raising public issues. Though he reveres the past, Costigan is very much a contemporary figure. His colleague in the history department, the late Professor W. Stull Holt, pointed out that "Giovanni has a larger reputation inside Washington State than out of it because he hasn't published much. Yet he writes exceptionally well. He is very retiring, sensitive and considerate. He has a tremendous sympathy, a sense of compassion for people, and it is ironical that he, of all people, was being hated by people." Holt was talking about the old days. Today, Giovanni is besieged by lecture invitations. When he reached mandatory retirement age in 1975, a tremendous groundswell of effort emerged to keep him actively at work. The Alumni Association stepped in and arranged for a series of evening Costigan lectures. He still attracts capacity audiences to Kane Hall in a room accommodating four hundred and fifty people. Through all of what I am saying, be it emphasized that I never became one of Giovanni's close friends. He would drop me a note once in a while if he liked something I had written, notes that I treasured, done in his tiny, precise script. To be truthful, I often feel uncomfortable with Giovanni. His graciousness is never failing, but being a scholar with a mind that will rank with any we may encounter in this century, he unintentionally gives one a feeling of inferiority. His questions are always probing, questing for more knowledge, and when you fail him by falling back on small talk, you sometimes say to yourself, "God, I have wasted my life with trivia."

One should never categorize friends. Too often, I believe, people slip into unconscious insularity by choosing only friends of like mind, drifting into a sort of suburbia of common interests and beliefs. I cannot imagine anyone more different from Giovanni Costigan in physical stature, demeanor, and view of the world than Rudi Becker. By his own reckoning, Rudi weighed seven stone eleven and stood nineteen hands high; certainly he was huge. He was bearded, burly and strong, and he had a deep, rich voice that sometimes shook the receiver when you picked up the telephone. He looked the way Paul Bunyan pictures did in my primary school books. To me, Rudi was the quintessential Seattleite.

Rudi Becker loved the salt air, Puget Sound, and the city which bred him. He was born in the Zindorf Apartments up at Seventh and James, one of those old buildings that barely escaped annihilation by the downtown freeway. Rudi knew every back alley, crevice, side street, offbeat place in the city. His father had worked as a waiter and maitre d' in most of the city's once-famous restaurants, places like Manca's, Chauncey Wright's, Blanc's and the Rathskeller—all of them gone, long gone. Rudi himself was many things. He was a tugboat skipper, a camp counselor, a contractor and builder, and for ten years he ran Harbor Tours on the waterfront. His friends were rich, big, small, poor, ordinary and often nutty. He liked newspaper guys and that was why he kept phoning in news items and ideas for my column.

These were not stories that would help him at all. He phoned in stuff about other people—a nice bartender, a business friend, a waitress down on her luck, a kid who needed help, or a cause worth mentioning. It went on, weeks and months, of almost daily phone calls from Rudi. Everywhere I went, people would say, "Hey, I saw that blurb in your column about the waterfront. You've been talking to Rudi again." Finally I couldn't stand it anymore, so I invited Rudi to lunch. "I'll pick you up," he said. He arrived in a six-year-old pickup truck; he was wearing a plaid shirt, boots and he had a drink in his hand. In this truck he had a glass holder, the kind that tilts, the kind they use on boats.

We settled in down at Ivar's and I asked him, "Why the hell do you do all this, all this phoning stuff in?" "I like to have a part in getting other people's stories in print," he said. "Maybe I'm a frustrated journalist. It must have started when I was a kid and got run over by a *P–I* delivery truck."

We became friends that day. Whenever I think of Rudi I remember Auntie Mame's great line, "Life is a feast, and most poor sons of bitches are starving to death!" Rudi said it differently: "It's a wonderful world, and anybody who doesn't like this life is crazy." And to Rudi Becker, the world was a wonderful place. He lived a sort of roaming life of fulfillment (God knows when he worked; he supported himself with some kind of siding and pre-fab business) in the back alleys and side streets of Seattle. He knew where to get things fixed, where to find a left-handed monkey wrench, how to get a friend out of jail; he knew the tides, the weather, the texture and the feel of the city. Ivar Haglund called him "some kind of genius. It was not that he knew so much about a little, but that he knew so much about so many things."

He was the "honorary mayor" of Carkeek Park, where he lived with his wife, Kay. Their home was a crazy, lovely hodgepodge of nautical collectibles, and it included many things Rudi had hand-crafted himself. But he was, even in his advancing age, a child of the streets—of the waterfront, the bars, the boats and the beaches. He roamed everywhere, missing nothing, lusting for precious fragments of joy the way some men collect jade, roaring with laughter at his own mischievous pranks.

Thus the phone would ring: "This is Rudi. I'm down here under the viaduct and some guy has scrawled a message on a pillar. It says, 'Joshua Green uses Medicare.' See ya later." One of Rudi's hobbies, if you can call it that, was what he called "giving people the mental hotfoot." He said he just "did things that were fun," but in his case, "fun" was a flexible word. He despised loud discourtesies, any form of boorish behavior, and his particular objects of scorn were people who impatiently honk horns behind you the instant a traffic light changes.

In one case, Rudi found himself stuck on the Ballard Bridge as cars lined up to await the passage of a boat. When the drawbridge barrier was lifted, one of the Unspeakables behind Rudi laid heavy on the horn. Calmly, Rudi (remember, he was seven stone eleven and stood nineteen hands) got out of his car and walked back to the honker's car. He deftly raised the fellow's hood, reached in and methodically ripped off the wires that connected the horn. Then he walked back to the spluttering driver. Towering above the honker he announced pleasantly: "There. Your horn was stuck, but now it's all fixed."

He had another method of enforcing courtesy among horn-honkers. Rudi used to drive a Packard convertible and this he equipped with a huge, old-fashioned blunderbuss, a fearsome looking weapon. Somehow he rigged it up to a very loud air horn. Not long after, at a downtown intersection, an impatient fellow in a top-down convertible behind, let go an angry blast at Rudi just as the light turned green. Rudi stood up in his own convertible. He reached down and picked up the gun. Deliberately and carefully, he held the gun high, squinted along the sights, then brought it slowly, methodically to dead aim on the horn-honker's chest.

The victim, of course, recoiled against his seat, a look of uncomprehending horror on his face. Then Rudi pulled the trigger. What resulted—a great loud air horn blast—shook up pedestrians for blocks. Rudi calmly sat down, put his car in gear, and drove off—leaving the poor wretch in a pallid state of near seizure. "Some people have to be taught to be nice to other people," he said later.

Most of Rudi's practical jokes had a message. Like many of us, he wearied of prattle about the "sportsmanship" and "responsibility" of experienced hunters. Scraping up a deer's head and hide (he knew exactly where to find them), he set out to prove a point. On the night before hunting season opened, he drove out along the highway, from which it is patently illegal to shoot at anything. Inside his deer head and hide he inserted the huge blade of an obsolete circular saw. At dawn, Rudi placed himself safely away from what he knew would be a line of fire. What followed was little short of carnage. "I damned near caused traffic accidents," he recalled. "Cars would screech to a stop and guys would jump out and start firing. Every clean shot let off a loud, metallic 'ping!' I counted fifteen bullet marks in that saw. Let 'em tell me about sportsmanship."

He once spread some Sea Dye along downtown Second Ave., and this being Seattle, he did not have to wait long for rain. Rudi happily watched the amazed faces around him as Second Ave. was transformed into a bright, glorious green. He used to carry raisins in a jar of soda water because he discovered that raisins, for some reason, move up and down in soda water.

"These," he would announce in a bar, or to some passerby on the street, "are very rare Chinese diving oysters. You see, the thing about Chinese diving oysters is that they feed by raising up and down in the water, collecting plankton." To his pleasure, he found a brisk market in selling Chinese diving oysters, charging what the traffic would bear. "It's funny," he reflected, "but I sure filled up a lot of Milk Fund bottles."

Back in 1976, Rudi said he would be checking into a hospital. We didn't hear from him for a few days so Carol Barnard, the column's curator and den mother, checked in at Rudi's house to see how he was doing. "Rudi isn't in the hospital yet," she reported. "He says to tell you that it isn't much. He says he has to get his automatic transmission repaired." Whatever it was, it was too much. Rudi died at the age of sixty-three.

The news, while it came as a shock, was no special cause for tears. Rudi didn't like tears, least of all for him. But there was a feeling of a tremendous, irreplaceable loss, because Rudi was uniquely "Seattle." He was the salt water Paul Bunyan, the questing, curious, small-town guy, a species becoming more rare as the late part of this century clanks on. When the news of his passing came, I called Ivar Haglund down at Pier 54. "Yeah, Rudi," Ivar said, sadly. "I remember one time he was down here on my dock talking to a visiting professor from New England, or someplace. They were standing at the rail, looking at the water and the sky on a clear summer night. They were talking about the solar system.

"When I closed up at about twelve-thirty, I left them standing on my dock, looking up at the stars, gesturing, talking and arguing. I had to come back early that morning about six o'clock and they were still there! Rudi and this scientist, talking about the sea, the sky and the solar system, on a beautiful morning with the sun shining over the water. That was Rudi Becker."

And in some strange way, it seems to me, that is Seattle.

10

Pillars in Pinstripes

"The very rich are different from you and me," said F. Scott Fitzgerald one time, and Mr. Hemingway replied, "Yes, they have more money." Each was probably oversimplifying, the way writers are prone to do. But the fact remains that the rich are different, because they do have more money, and frequently, like pool hall Democrats and other low types with common interests, they tend to be a bad influence on each other.

Frankly, I don't know much about the Seattle Establishment. I know what color they are. I know their suits probably come from Littler. I know that they live in the Highlands, Washington Park, Hunts Point, Medina, Magnolia and Broadmoor. I know that they belong to the Rainier Club (usually), that they join the Seattle Tennis Club (frequently), that they support Seattle Opera and the symphony and attend some performances (reluctantly). I also know that when they get mad at the unions or sick of our winter weather, they feel compelled to fly away to Palm Springs and tear off a few rounds of golf.

Over the years I have heard some of them express the nervous opinion that the *Seattle Times* is getting too racy or liberal. They have little to fear. The late Longacres mogul and founder, Joe Gottstein, who was sort of an Establishment unto himself, once said of Seattle's Establishmentarians, would-be and otherwise: "They are nice enough people, but they do all of their drinking and screwing at home." Joe meant that they were low-key and private. Joe was right.

Back in the mid-sixties, a wealthy Seattleite, Stimson Bullitt, too much the maverick to be a team-playing Establishmentarian himself, founded *Seattle* magazine. In an early issue the editors sought to delineate Seattle's Establishment. This was the right magazine to take on the job. It was staffed by young, mostly well-born imports from the east, who could get into places like the Tennis Club without forcing the waiters to keep a wary eye on the silverware.

The magazine compiled an impressive list of names who belonged, or had playing privileges, in the Seattle Establishment. Out of about one hundred and sixty people named in this article, I counted up the number I actually knew. The total was twenty-one. Of fourteen ladies the magazine listed as "grandes dames," I didn't know a single one. Most of them I'd never heard of.

This compilation is not set down in a spirit of inverse snobbery. It just happens that I run—as most writers do—on a muddier track than they do. For many years I was a sportswriter, which meant that the free booze in jock culture was poured in a less genteel environment than theirs. Later, when I moved out of sports into a more general column, one of the

Establishment referred to me as a "knee-pants Winchell." There are a few insults one treasures.

So it is not, to repeat, inverse snobbery or any strain of plebian resentment that kept me from mingling with the Establishment. It is just that we had little in common—an irrelevant point anyway, since in Seattle society's verdant pastures, the fact was established long ago that I am the social equivalent of a dull thud. Moreover, you will not get many rungs up on anyone's social ladder when much of your adult life is spent verifying the demographics and arithmetical dictums of the infield fly rule.

"Committee rosters serve Establishmentologists in the same way that May Day photographs of the reviewing stand above Lenin's Tomb serve Kremlinologists." The quote is from Richard Rovere's acclaimed essay, "The American Establishment." Seattle, perhaps more than most cities, has an almost celestial reverence toward committees. We also are big on early morning meetings, the kinds often inspired by prayer and incantation. As for Rovere's analogy of a reviewing stand, this is of only marginal help in Seattle: our Establishmentarians tend to be self-effacing men.

Of the twenty-one Establishment figures I knew at the time of *Seattle* magazine's roll call, subtract a few who may have cashed out via Bonney-Watson (an Establishment embalming firm), then add a dozen or so I've met in the past few years. That still is not an impressive total. I cannot count any of them as more than casual friends or acquaintances. Any other knee-pants Winchell could have done better.

Seattle magazine made a strong—I think valid—point that Seattle's Establishment is egalitarian, at least in a social sense: "Most newcomers are quickly invited to the best parties, providing they (1) are reasonably well-educated (an Ivy League background is a huge plus); (2) like to ski, sail or play golf (in that order); (3) have 'interesting' or respectable jobs (Boeing is not a plus, but private-school teaching, law, medicine and architecture are—in that order), and (4) they are reasonably attractive and well-spoken (strong views are a decided drawback, unless voiced with great tact.)" When *Seattle* magazine's sociological safari ran its course, the editors decided that Seattle's Establishment "includes those individuals whose ideas, tastes and energy have a major influence on the community, yet by no means does it include everyone who fits that description. What distinguishes the Seattle Establishment is that it operates behind the scenes, and its members are cautious (they would say 'judicious')."

And a University of Washington sociologist once likened Seattle's Establishment to the Cascade mountain range: "It represents nothing so much as a series of separated peaks which are partially visible some of the time and completely visible none of the time."

A look at the half-dozen or so people who own the Seattle Seahawks football team provides a glimpse of what the local Establishment is. And to emphasize the character of the Seattle Seahawks owners it is necessary to take a look at their opposite numbers who own football teams in other cities. The Los Angeles Rams were once owned by four people, one of whom, Daniel Reeves, would not speak to two of the others. The fourth owner was Bob Hope, America's friend, and therefore immune to such feuds. These people were immortalized as "The Fighting Owners." As for Reeves, he made history of sorts when he fueled up on Haig & Haig, then called up his coach at 3:00 A.M. and fired him. This set an NFL record that has not been matched to this day.

In St. Louis, William and Charles Bidwell, a couple of

eminent Establishmentarians, inherited the city's team from their mother. They developed a sibling rivalry and parted bitterly. Owners of the Minnesota Vikings, notably Bernard Ridder, the newspaper tycoon, and Max Winter, another Establishmentarian, hate each other's guts. The multiple ownership of the New England Patriots has been split down the middle like the 97th Congress, while the Oakland Raiders reached their present efficiency after loudly publicized internecine warfare at the owner-management level. At this writing, Oakland's managing general partner, Al Davis, definitely a non-Establishmentarian, threatens to commit legal genocide against his NFL partners.

All sports franchises tend to float, which is to say that they move about like a tolerated big money craps game. Baseball owners, especially, are reminiscent of the Bakhtiari tribes in Persia, herding their livestock through vast transhumance journeys, from one lush pasture to another. Many of the Establishmentarian nabobs of the NFL own teams in one city and live in another.

Into this big-bucks bacchanal of compulsive nomadism, feuds, finance and fine Scotch stepped the group of Seattle Seahawks owners. Together they paid $16 million for the Seahawks franchise and they are unique in the history of big-time professional sports—because most of them genuinely believe it is "good service to the community to have a team."

Almost all of these owners graduated from Seattle public schools and went on to attend the University of Washington. All of their business offices are within one square mile of Fourth and Pike. Most belong to the same clubs, deal with the same banks, see each other at the same parties, can be found at the same cultural and charity ventures; each supports, to a greater or lesser degree, the Seattle Downtown

Development Association and assorted arts groups, often of their wives' choosing.

They all share, in large part, the Establishmentarian values of Seattle's business community. Each, in his own way, has kept a low profile, shunning the limelight, surfacing only when necessary for the doing of good works. Impeccable behavior; solid, dependable, a bit dull. If by the wildest chance one of them felt the urge to fire the football coach at 3:00 A.M., somebody would have to set the alarm clock to awaken him into action.

Perhaps the best known of these owners is David E. (Ned) Skinner, a tall, congenial fellow, with a compulsion for taking on difficult civic tasks the way a confirmed horse player cannot resist betting on a horse which has not won a race in its last fourteen outings. "Skinner," wrote David Brewster one time, "seems to have an uncanny nose for finding tasks with impossible odds." Thus it was Skinner who once took on the thankless task of heading something called the Seattle–King County Economic Development Council, a group which devoted itself (with some success, largely due to Ned's efforts) to diversifying the region's economy after Boeing blew a gasket in the 1969–70 recession. He was the underwriting fundraiser for the Seattle World's Fair. As Brewster tells it, Skinner once tried to interest a local capitalist in joining him to save the Seattle Pilots, which were bankrupt and about to be whisked out of town. The man protested that he did not have the slightest interest in baseball. "Good," replied Skinner, "all the more reason. Now you can finally do your civic duty."

A prominent Seattle attorney once told me, "If Seattle didn't have a Ned Skinner, we would have to invent him." So when Ned Skinner tells you, as he said to me one time, that the reason he invested in the Seahawks was because he felt it would be "nice for the city" to have a pro football team, you can believe him. He also invested in the original Seattle Sounders franchise, before he had ever seen a soccer game, except on television. That, too, he thought, would be a nice idea for the city.

You can also believe Howard S. Wright, the construction man, who didn't think football was much of an investment. "But since we have the good fortune of living in Seattle," he said, "I felt it was time we stepped up and pledged a responsibility to the community." Another is Lynn Himmelman, retired chairman and chief executive officer of Western International Hotels (before it became gelded into Westin). Himmelman acts as "sort of an agent" for a group of smaller investors in the Seahawks.

At the time, none of the Seahawks' new owners really thought football was a good investment and they probably still don't, even though television revenue and big crowds have made the Seahawks profitable. "If this were just another business venture," another of the partners, Monte Bean, told me, "I wouldn't need that. As an investment, football is less than attractive. But if it turns out okay, we should have some fun and satisfaction." The only person in the entire group with any real background in professional sports is Herman Sarkowsky, who can be described as only semi-Establishment.

And finally, there is the Nordstrom family. As Bean recalls it, Sarkowsky was scheduled to be the majority owner, putting up 51 percent of the money. But when the unexpectedly high franchise price of $16 million was announced, Sarkowsky said, "Hey, guys, I can't do it." Then the quiet, polite voice of Lloyd Nordstrom was heard. "Maybe we can do something as a family," he ventured. "That settled it," said Bean. "The only other guy heavy enough in our group to handle it was Ned, and he didn't want to make a lifetime career out of football."

That was more than six years ago, and the Seahawk owners, as in the Cascade mountains analogy, have remained partly visible some of the time and completely visible none of the time. Lloyd Nordstrom passed away before the Seahawks played their first game; he was a man of uncommon dignity and charm. The role of managing partner recently passed from Sarkowsky to Elmer Nordstrom, the family patriarch. Elmer is so modest that, even as managing partner, and therefore the presumed authoritative spokesman for the team, he is reluctant to discuss any franchise business with sportswriters. After victorious Seahawks games, I have often watched Elmer standing alone in the dressing room, beaming and happy; I sometimes wonder if the players even know who he is.

By observing the Nordstrom family, you learn a little more about Seattle and its Establishment. Like many other Establishmentarians, this family started out poor and came down rich rather late in the going. The family business began in 1901 when John Nordstrom, a Swedish immigrant, teamed up with a man named Wallin, a shoe repairman, to open a shoe store. John's three sons, Everett, Elmer and Lloyd, grew up on a farm in Rainier Valley, and together they bought out Wallin for $30,000 apiece in 1929 without much hope that the original shoe store could support all three of them.

When I was a kid, Elmer Nordstrom used to fit my shoes, a claim that hundreds of Seattle people can make. It still is a company policy that all Nordstroms, scheduled to be active in the family business, must work in the store, dealing with customers, knowing their needs, and hearing their complaints. The Nordstroms are a close-knit clan and the family is dedicated to Swedish virtues of hard work, modesty and privacy. The working clan now includes Elmer, John and Bruce Nordstrom, and Jack McMillan, who married Lloyd and Illsley Nordstrom's daughter, Loyal. By 1960, Nordstrom was the largest shoe store in the country, probably in the world. In the sixties, the Nordstroms expanded their business into apparel and clothing accessories, and today Nordstrom stores represent the largest specialty-clothing chain on the West Coast. So work-conscious are the Nordstroms that for a long time they did not join downtown service clubs "because the lunches were too long."

I used to struggle with the necessary business of reading newspaper society columns when we had such things. The doings and flittings of Establishmentarian wives, it seemed to me, involved mostly charity work and aimless luncheons and parties. Once, in the sixties, my publisher, Dan Starr, got the notion that I should run more names—meaning influential names—in my column. This was swell by me for one main reason—no columnist ever has too many items to fill the daily "news hole" given over to such trivia. To set up my own Fifth Column in the Establishment, I hired Laura Gilmore, who had earlier retired from the *P-I*'s then-called society section, and Laura phoned in stuff on a free-lance basis. Even today, Laura retains an encyclopedic knowledge of the doings, goings, comings and idiosyncrasies of the Seattle Establishment. I am afraid I stretched Laura's patience at times, because too often, when she phoned in a news note, Laura would find it a necessary tedium to explain to me who the hell she was talking about. The experiment died after a short time—to my vast relief, and I'm sure to Laura's.

A Leonard Lyons or a Walter Winchell would starve to death in Seattle; the city has no flamboyant, colorful, wealthy cafe society performers in its midst. Its Establishment, I have always argued, should be referred to as "middle-class millionaires." Seattle's staid, middle-class traditions, among both rich and poor, once led the famed publicist, Tex McCrary, to remark, "I always think of Seattle as a place where the town's only call girl has a pull-down bed."

The local Establishment is quite weak on lineage, since Seattle, in a figurative sense, has scarcely wiped the pitch bark off its lumber origins. Many of the recognized Establishment members are self-made men; I would guess that a fair percentage of them tend to stand before mirrors and privately admire their own handiwork. It always was a smug city in many ways.

An exception is Eddie Carlson. No man in Seattle's history ever started lower and went higher into the Seattle Establishment than this one-time page-boy-bell-hop-desk-clerk-parking-lot-attendant, who was graduated from Lincoln High School in 1928. He has been called the "Grand Sachem" of the downtown business scene, and it has been said that Eddie is the "single most important guy in this town to have on your side if you want to get a big civic project off the ground."

Take a look at him and wonder how this man, now in his early seventies, did not die of overwork. Before he left Seattle to become head of United Airlines, he was the driving force that raised Western International Hotels from a small regional hotel chain into the world's third largest combine of hostelries. During this time—when Eddie Carlson traveled as much as 100,000 miles a year—he became Seattle's most influential Establishmentarian.

From 1955 to 1966, Eddie Carlson served successively as chairman of the World's Fair Commission, president and chairman of the Century 21 Exposition, and president of the Pacific Science Center Foundation. It was also Eddie Carlson, visiting Brussels one time, who sketched out on a restaurant napkin the rough design of what would later become the Space Needle.

He began as a parking lot attendant at the old Mount Baker ski lodge. He worked for a while as a page boy—in the memorable style, one likes to think, of Johnny's "Call for Phil-lip Morris!"—at the old Ben Franklin Hotel while going to the University of Washington. He worked his way up to elevator boy, then night bellhop, after which he quit to go into an ill-starred venture selling hat-blocking equipment. Later he hopped bells at the Roosevelt Hotel; then, after shipping out to sea on the President Lincoln for eight months (during which time he made up his university courses by correspondence), he returned to hold down jobs as a desk clerk in some quite forgettable Northwest hotels. During one interlude he was the manager of the President Hotel in Mount Vernon and worked weekends as a fry cook in Bellingham. After that, excepting a hitch in the navy in World War II, Eddie Carlson's rise to the presidency of Western International Hotels had an uninterrupted Algeresque flavor.

I did a couple of stories on Eddie and found his rise to Establishmenthood to be exasperatingly lacking in color. But he is a warm and engaging fellow. He is short, with thick curly hair, a broad mouth that smiles readily, and he wears thick horn-rimmed glasses. In demeanor, he gives the impression that he has just accepted an appointment as registrar at a small mid-western university. But Eddie Carlson has dominated board rooms for most of his adult life. Today he sits on a

fistful of boards, including those of Univar, Virginia Mason
Medical Foundation and the 5th Avenue Theatre Association.

He made such a hit with United Airlines, turning its deep
red ink into black, that prestigious *Fortune* magazine took
note of him in a lengthy profile. At one point in his research,
the *Fortune* writer came to see Gordon Bass, one of Carlson's
early compatriots at Western International Hotels. "I've
been all over this city," he said, "interviewing dozens of
people about Carlson. Isn't there anyone who has anything
bad to say about the guy?" "Keep looking," Bass laughed,
"but you won't find one."

There could be something about Eddie Carlson that you
won't like, and I may be it. You see, I first met Eddie Carlson
under an unusual circumstance. At that time—in 1956—a
bunch of restaurateurs wanted to start what they called "an
around-town column," meaning they wanted somebody to
chronicle "the action" in and around Seattle. About the
only real action a determined livewire could find in those
bland days was a spot of illegal fishing. But it was felt, by the
restaurateurs, at least, that if somebody wrote about downtown doings, it might give people the impression that the
sidewalks weren't pulled up at 6:00 P.M.

The group, as I recall, included Vic Rosellini, Johnny
Franco and Cliff Warling. But they got together fourteen
or fifteen other restaurant guys, including Eddie Carlson,
who then bossed the Olympic Hotel, with its Olympic
Grill and its Golden Lion. The idea was that they would
buy space, the column would run next to their ads, and
they would give me ten dollars each. Even I was smart
enough to know that this nifty little scam would send the
managing editor exploding through the North Pole of the

P–I globe. So an arrangement was made that they would pay the paper, then the paper would pay me, in a single sum added onto my regular weekly check, for the extra work of the column.

I was still working in the jock shop, or sports department, full time then, but I was dying to try something else. I desperately wanted that column because I could see it as a way out of dressing-room interviews and the repetitive stuff that makes up the average sports page. But even this above-board scheme, it seemed then, would not meet approval from the *P–I* management. "Call Eddie Carlson," I told the originators of this plan. "If I get Eddie on my side, I know this thing will work."

So the first time I met Eddie Carlson was over lunch at the Golden Lion. We talked at great length about the idea, and I explained how newspaper guys were always thought to be on the take from promoters, businessmen or travel bureaus, and how I would have enough trouble getting into heaven without a rap like that. I explained to Eddie (and to the others) how I would probably go out of my way not to mention their establishments; that if they got any good out of it, it would be that people might come downtown under the impression that something was, indeed, going on besides watching some of the better peep shows on First Ave. Eddie quickly understood all this, and that was the beginning of our friendship.

Later I went back to the *P–I* and laid out the plan. "Eddie Carlson is all for this," I said, pushing truth to its outer limits. I knew that Eddie was the best trump card I had. I'm not sure if that sold the rather shaky scheme, but I have a hunch Eddie may have said something to Charley Lindeman, the publisher, so we were off in a blaze of bromides and cliches. The restaurant guys pulled out after a couple of years, but we all had what we wanted. They had somebody to write about the city and I made it over the wall out of sports.

This meant that the readers, or those so inclined to pony up the price of a *P–I*, have been subjected to an overkill of my words for the past twenty-six years. And if that adds up to saying something bad about Eddie Carlson, go ahead. Maybe he deserves it.

I'm not even sure if Harold Shefelman was given an Establishment pedigree by *Seattle* magazine, but he certainly was a major influence on the community. I have not seen him in years—now in his eighties, he lives quietly in semi-retirement—but I remember him as rather short, square set, round of face and immensely strong and fit.

The name Shefelman has never been exactly a household word in Seattle. Nevertheless, he sat on the University of Washington Board of Regents from 1957 to 1975; he was a prime mover in bringing Charles Odegaard to Seattle as president of the university, and it is doubtful if that school ever had a better top man than Odegaard. Henry Suzzalo might have come close. Shefelman was the acknowledged authority on university finances, and as chairman of the regents' Metropolitan Tract Committee, he had tremendous influence over Seattle's most valuable ten acres of land.

Shefelman was a bonding lawyer and he knew where the money was. He was bond counsel to the Washington Toll Bridge Authority. It was Shefelman who sold the $30 million in bonds that were needed to finance the Evergreen Point Bridge. He once headed a $500,000 drive to raise money for Seattle Pacific University. He was, according to one news reporter, "the prime organizer of all the community factions that came together to create the Seattle Center, and before that he played a big role in finance planning for the Seattle World's Fair." The sportswriters used to spoof him a lot in satiric skits at their mid-winter sports banquet, and somebody hung the sobriquet on him, "Harold Shufflecard." Nevertheless, be it noted that much of what we take for granted in Seattle today (most of it good) came about because of Harold Shefelman, a man few would recognize on the street.

For a long time the most visible figure in Seattle's Establishment was another bonding lawyer—Jim Ellis. He never sought the limelight, but because of the spectacular, politicized nature of his work, Jim Ellis naturally was thrust into the public arena. Ellis has been called "a sort of one-man radar for impending urban crises" by Joel Connelly, a hard-line journalist on the subject of environment. "He spotted crises," wrote Connelly, "usually several years in advance, and designed programs to meet them."

It is a truism—recognized by too few people—that danger signs on the horizon are usually spotted by the intelligentsia, whose unread research papers and dry reports foretell the shape of things in years to come. One should remember this, each time we hear derisive statements about pointy-headed intellectuals who should be kept out of practical affairs and remain in their ivory towers and research labs. Yet it is the scientists in botany who give us signals on food supplies, sociologists who study mass behavior patterns and warn us of a shift in population—things that may give us much anguish in the future. It so happened that one of these, Dr. W.T. Edmondson, in the University of Washington's Department of Zoology, was the man who gave Jim Ellis the voice of scientific authority he required. For what had to be accomplished, each needed the other.

Because of Dr. Edmondson's studies—which showed that

Lake Washington would one day become "dead," a body of water both odiferous and dangerous—Jim Ellis became a moral and intellectual force who changed the shape of a city and a region that was hell-bent on imitating large eastern metropolitan centers—cities which today are still trying to extricate themselves from dirt, blight, slop and despair, the inevitable harvest of neglect. For more than twenty years, Ellis became the catalyst, the driving force in a common crusade that would, one day, promote Seattle to first rank among American cities.

These are simple things to say of a man, when such things are said in retrospect. But when you read the words, then envision them in action, you find that spotting a crisis, setting up a design to solve it, then whipping others into action, takes months and years of difficult, energy-draining commitment, the kind of public work that few scientists could handle. So with the help of Dr. Edmondson, Jim Ellis gave up much of his working life to a Seattle that now preens itself in such accolades as "America's most livable city."

In line with most of his Establishment brethren, Jim Ellis was Seattle-raised and educated. He grew up out on 50th Ave. S., near where it intersects with Genesee St., and as a kid, he played and swam in Lake Washington. He went to Franklin High School, then Yale, and returned to Seattle to get his law degree at the University of Washington. As a young lawyer he did a hitch as a deputy prosecutor for Chuck Carroll in the King County prosecutor's office.

It would be nice and tidy to record that young Ellis met up with Dr. Edmondson, then abruptly took off in a blaze of crusading fervor. It was more a case of two people, both alarmed by the putrid future of Lake Washington, having the same goal. When Jim Ellis started in law practice, one of his first clients was a small sewer district out in Bryn Mawr, a bit south of Rainier Beach and abutting the city of Renton. He was sitting on the porch at the home of Sam Kenney, a Bryn Mawr sewer commissioner, looking out over the south tip of Lake Washington. "You know, it's crazy," he said to Sam. "You and I could hit that Boeing sewer treatment plant and Renton's sewer treatment plant with a 22-calibre rifle from your front porch. Yet you have to build another treatment plant for Bryn Mawr."

That was in the early fifties. Jim Ellis began reading and thinking and it came to him then that many of our problems—air pollution, water pollution, public transportation—can't be solved by one city acting alone. As we grow and spread and populate ourselves into what is called Pugetopolis, the bell begins to toll. And you do not send to know for whom the bell tolls, because in due time the damned bell will rattle your eardrums. During this period and long before, Dr. Edmondson was doing his research on Lake Washington. The critical part of it surfaced under the title, "Eutrophication of Lake Washington," which meant quite simply that sewage treatment plants and sometimes raw sewage were over-fertilizing the lake. Algae soon would be thick in its waters. What Edmondson knew, as a matter of scientific certainty, was that if we didn't stop dumping sewage into Lake Washington, the water would choke on algae and we would be driving to work with clothespins on our noses.

Dr. Edmondson's report was what Jim Ellis needed. He had to have something with authority, a study with the stamp of science on it, to convince people the bell was getting louder. By then, Ellis was working as counsel to the Municipal League, because he needed the hundred dollars a month it paid. He got the Municipal League turned on, and finally, a thing called the Metropolitan Area Problems Committee was formed. (An early member of that committee was a young engineer named Dan Evans.) By now, Ellis was deeper and deeper into something that would, in a profound way, dominate the rest of his life.

One of the charms of democracy—and one of its exasperations—is that each town council, each committee, each city government, is an ego unto itself; this ego is the sum of many individual egos, prejudices, beliefs and even torpors. So Ellis, and those he rallied with him, went out on the revival circuit, so to speak, to try and open a lot of closed-door minds. Ellis alone gave hundreds of speeches, answered thousands of questions; he went to Renton, Bellevue, Lake Hills, Mercer Island, Lake City, Kirkland, Bothell—everywhere he could go to whip up citizen interest in saving Lake Washington. He pleaded with council people, church people and ate enough service club luncheons to destroy the stomach of a healthy horse.

He was winning, but it wasn't easy. Our Puget Sound version of rednecks rose up against him. The far-righters denounced his program of area-wide cooperation as "communism in disguise." They spread rumors that a "city slicker" was out to take the small communities. One such obstructionist actually got himself on television and ate some algae, just to prove that the stuff in Lake Washington "wouldn't hurt anybody."

The first vote in the first effort to create Metro, an umbrella superagency over cities in King County, came in March 1958. The measure asked the voters of individual cities to approve sewage disposal, transportation and planning. It passed in Seattle, but in some of the surrounding communities, notably Kent, Auburn, Kirkland, Highline and Redmond, it went down to defeat. The Metro measure was resubmitted that fall, but this time the transportation and planning segments were dropped, and the issue was solely a drive to clean up Lake Washington. Cities south and away from the lake also were dropped, and the campaign centered that summer only on cities in the Lake Washington basin.

One marvels, at times, how fate smiles on this beautiful region. That summer of 1958, as it happens, was one of the driest in years. Lake Washington sank by more than four feet. And because of this dry weather, the stench of algae, now abundant on the shores, could be noticed from Renton to Kirkland, from Leschi to Mercer Island. A voter can vote with his feet, but he can also vote with his nose. The measure, which created the superagency of Metro, passed handily.

Dr. Edmondson had promised, "If we get the sewage out of there, the lake will be as clean as it was in 1931," the year when the spoilage of Lake Washington began. It was a promise delivered, for the once-murky lake waters, which gave a visible depth of only three feet, soon became clear to a depth of fifteen and twenty feet, even deeper than that. By 1970, civic leaders drank a toast to success—with clean Lake Washington water.

Whether or not the toast was drunk to Ellis is a bit hazy at this distance; no matter. Long before that, in the mid-sixties, the square-set, dogged bond lawyer was busy on yet another, bolder, bigger and more imaginative program. Ellis was cranking up again. His blueprint was a giant, multi-purpose King County spending program that ultimately would total some $850 million dollars, a program known as Forward Thrust. By now Ellis himself was at the edge of the Seattle Establishment; if he wasn't part of it, at least he was trusted by it. He first unveiled his bold plan to Eddie Carlson, then head of Western International Hotels; William Allen, president of Boeing; Walter Straley, president of Pacific Northwest Bell, and Bill Jenkins, of Seattle-First National Bank. They were Establishmentarians all, and to a man they bought the Ellis plan.

Ellis demanded and got $50,000 for administrative staff help before he would begin. Then began a careful program of selling the rest of the downtown business establishment, as well as newspapers and television stations, on a plan that eventually changed the entire face of Seattle and King County. Ellis was always, in his own words, "a bit mavericky" for the conservative business establishment. And he likes to recall that one of them said, "It looks to me like you're asking us to drive the nails in our own coffins." At which point Eddie Carlson replied coolly, "It isn't that at all. This thing is going to go. Do you want to be in on the act, or out of it?"

Ellis first revealed his grandiose program in a landmark speech to the downtown Seattle Rotary Club. It was not a speech full of redolent phrases or inspiring invocations, but it was a word of warning—and the numbers shook everyone. He proposed that some $500 million be spent on rapid transit, a domed stadium, parks, green belts, street improvements and a world trade center. Of this, some $200 million would be asked of King County voters, the rest coming from federal sources. Before it ended, the total came to $709.5 million and King County residents voted by more than 60 percent to tax themselves to the tune of $333.9 million.

Largely because of Jim Ellis, the Seattle Establishment "came on board," as businessmen are fond of saying about anyone who half agrees with a principle. The outcome at the beginning was far from certain. And for Ellis himself, it was more endless meetings, more cajoling, more politicking, and he found, of course, that the rubber chicken lunches had not measurably improved since 1958. This time he would drive himself to the point of broken health. There are literally hundreds of people, to be sure, who deserve credit for the Forward Thrust program, most of which passed in February, 1968. But it was Ellis, with his track record on Lake Washington, who was the central figure in putting these disparate groups together. In the year of the Forward Thrust campaign, Ellis worked day and night, taking only three Sundays off, before the February election. He entered a hospital shortly thereafter, suffering from a serious stomach ulcer and physical exhaustion.

It was not all victory. The rapid transit bond issue failed, and somewhere along the line the world trade center was forgotten. But out of it came the Kingdome, which brought to the region major league sports on a scale enjoyed by few other American cities. Even more important today, Forward Thrust projects can be found in every corner of King County. With Forward Thrust came more than four thousand acres of new park lands and fifty-three miles of waterfront for public use. A multiplicity of parks, new, old and revitalized, came to the region; trails, such as the now-popular Burke-Gilman Trail came into being; swimming pools and tennis courts, new playfields and boat launching sites, recreation centers and open spaces began to proliferate throughout the 1970s.

With Forward Thrust came the Seattle Aquarium, Marymoor Park in Redmond, Fort Dent Athletic Center in Tukwila, Luther Burbank park on Mercer Island; Woodland Park Zoo, because of improvements, now ranks among the top five zoos in the country. Rapid transit was defeated, to be sure, but out of Forward Thrust we got the county-wide

Metro transit system, now acknowledged as a model in the nation. With Forward Thrust the city is now enhanced by the planting of trees and shrubs, and underground wiring has beautified many of our neighborhoods. More than two hundred miles of improved arterial streets came out of Forward Thrust, so did thirteen new fire stations, a King County Youth Services Center, 130 small, but important, neighborhood improvement programs—the list can go on.

And if you happen to be sitting in the sunshine in Freeway Park, listening to the free summer concerts, enjoying a well-designed open space in the heart of a great city—well, that too came from Forward Thrust.

Jim Ellis still is a young, vigorous man of sixty, but the years have not been kind. His wife, Mary Lou, is seriously ill with diabetes. Ellis has taken what amounts to a leave of absence from his law firm. He has resigned from all committees and public service bodies. "My father," his son told me recently, "spends almost twenty-four hours a day caring for my mother. He has devoted himself to her the same way he devoted himself to his community—all out, nothing held back."

The next time a national magazine, or a book, places Seattle among the top-ranked cities in America, as it surely will do, it is good to remember why that is. It is because of Jim Ellis.

11

Purple and White

The first time I saw Charlie Russell he was wearing a white football helmet. He had on a faded practice jersey, his black legs were bare, and Charlie's team, Garfield, was there to play West Seattle in a practice game on a warm September afternoon at Hiawatha Playfield. Memories are tricky, unless you are a computer, but I have this vivid recollection of Charlie Russell's white helmet, weaving and swaying, somehow staying above the crashing, moving bodies, some trying to protect him, others trying to converge and smash him down.

This may be a corny way to describe a football player; still, in retrospective memory, Charlie's white helmet seemed like a single dominant chrysanthemum, bowing and veering in a breeze, alone above the shrubbery below. Yes, that's corny enough. But Charlie ran that way, now shifting, now leaping, twisting and spinning, moving in a violent rhythm that excited the senses, the way a great ballet dancer can leave an audience breathless.

This long ago September afternoon was also the first time I ever saw Leon Brigham up close. By then—it was 1934— Brigham already was a legend in Seattle high school athletics. He was thin of frame, his dark hair receded slightly; he wore light, metal-rimmed glasses, and affected a thin, neatly-clipped moustache, which gave the over-all effect of a stern office superintendent or a singularly unemotional bureau-crat.

Why does one remember things like this?

Memories, human memory, cannot be programmed, filed and called up at will. Like all of us, I am plagued by visual instant replays of times past; a chance remark, a fearful moment, a time of intense embarrassment, a brief sorrow, a long-gone moment of laughter—fragments spaced crazily in a patchwork of recollection, all of which, surely, have some reason for permanent existence in the subconscious mind. I only know that my first sight of Charlie Russell running with a football and Leon Brigham moving intently along the sidelines made a strong impression on me at the time. It could be—or maybe I just like to believe so—that Charlie Russell and Brigham's team, composed of other black kids and Japanese players, caused me to think more about a wider world beyond the confines of West Seattle.

A year after I first saw him in that football game, I played in a baseball game against Charlie Russell. It was a close game in which West Seattle beat Garfield, and when it ended I made my way through players of both teams leaving the field and confronted Charlie Russell. "Nice game, Charlie," I said, extending a hand. His round, black face, fixed with disap-pointment, brightened momentarily. He accepted the handshake and said, "Thank you, thank you." It was only later that a singular fact occurred to me—Charlie Russell was the first black person I had ever spoken with or touched.

Many years passed before I met Leon Brigham—not until 1943, when the *P–I* sent me out to write up the story of a high school football game. I just hung around the paper in those days, by no means on its payroll, and Harold Torbergson, who covered prep sports, asked if I'd like to drive out to West Seattle Stadium, where Garfield was playing that afternoon. Torby gave me a quick course on how to keep a running account of a football game. He showed me how to type up the starting lineups, record substitutions, and add up the significant statistics. My first brush with Leon Brigham came when I knocked on Garfield's dressing room door. Brigham himself opened the door, surveyed me as though I were an interloping mischief-maker, and he snapped, "What do you want?" I said I was from the *P–I* and could I have Garfield's starting lineup? "Wait out there," he said, shutting the door. In a few minutes a student manager came out and handed me a hand-written lineup sheet.

Please accept this coincidence: the first time I ever met Leon Brigham involved the first story I ever wrote in a newspaper. It was a story that ran no more than four column inches long, but it was the first tasty, heady wine of authorial celebrity. It didn't even have a byline. But it was my story, I had written it, and it got by the editor's pencil almost unscathed. You remember things like that. I also remember that I had to resist an impulse to stop people on the street, show them the pitifully small story and say, "Hey, look at this, I wrote it."

For such ill-described reasons, yet vividly impressionistic in memory, I began to realize that there was a part of Seattle much different in tone and color from any I had known as a boy. The first sight of Charlie Russell, recklessly graceful in a meaningless practice game; the first close look at Leon Brigham, and later our brief, cold encounter—had an effect I can't fully explain. Since that time Garfield High School, by no means a typical Seattle school, has held a special fascination. I have never been inside its building, but the school had such a strange, distant effect on me, on how I think about Seattle, that I am compelled to write about it.

It is true, perhaps, that old Broadway High School can boast a longer roster of "distinguished alums"—it is a formidable list. It surely is true that Roosevelt, Lincoln, Queen Anne, Cleveland and Ballard graduated kids who contributed greatly to the city. The same measure can be applied to my own schools, West Seattle and Franklin. It is the deserved harvest a city accepts, having paid for, and supported, good public schools. Other cities are not so fortunate.

But Garfield was, and is today, like no other school in Seattle. Consider its location: Garfield sits up there on 23rd Ave., a few blocks from the central city, ringed closely on all sides by a largely black community. The stores and shops and restaurants are run by blacks. The black district expands eastward, and down into what was known, in more benighted times, as "coon hollow." To the south and west of Garfield is Seattle's old Chinatown, now refurbished and known as the International District. Farther to the east, above what we now call the "central area," the color grows rapidly more white and the incomes correspondingly higher. This area comprises neighborhoods of Washington Park and Madrona, and further toward the lake, Madison Park and Leschi, also Broadmoor, an enclave that still is determinedly walled-in and prosperously private. Many of Seattle's Jewish families can be found in Madrona and Washington Park (precious few in Broadmoor), so that Garfield High School, sitting in the middle of all this, has long been a blend of cultural, ethnic and economic disparity.

This rich mixture of color and background, with its obvious extremes in parental wealth, is Garfield's trademark. Even before the "magnet" and "option" programs—which draw gifted students to Garfield from all over the city—the school produced many top scholars. Viewing this mixture, one is forever pleased, even faintly surprised, that Garfield has maintained such intense unity, its celebrated us-against-them competitive school spirit. Nobody is quite sure how it happened. For as many years as I can recall, it has been said that "Garfield always had outstanding teachers." Perhaps that is part of the reason. Another part may be that the school's first principal (when it was founded in 1920 as East High) was George N. Porter, a far-sighted man with a gift for building that nebulous thing known as "school spirit" into his young high school. What becomes most clear is Mr. Porter was either remarkably prescient or extremely lucky—perhaps both—when he hired Leon Brigham as his first athletic coach in 1921.

Brigham came from the Midwest, where he had been assistant athletic director at the University of Iowa. He didn't even have a teaching certificate when he first was interviewed by Porter, who also was interested in building up his school's music program. His first question to Brigham was, "Can you sing?" and Brigham replied, "Hell, no. If I have to sing I guess you can count me out." But he got the job (taking courses at the University of Washington to get his teaching certificate) and for the first few years he coached all major sports—basketball, track, baseball and football. Initially, Brigham's teams played only at the freshman and sophomore levels. But in 1922, Garfield's first football season in varsity competition, Brigham gave a warning signal of what was to come. Garfield went up against a splendid Franklin squad, a championship team with all its stars returning. Brig's kids—not a senior among them—held Franklin to a scoreless tie.

It took more years to build, but by 1927, Brigham began to reshape the record books on high school sports in Seattle. His basketball champions of 1927 became known as the "wonder team." It featured such players as Rocky Moore, Hank Swanson, Dutch Schaab, Marty Backer and Bill Sims. This team never lost a game. It was never behind in a game. On some occasions, it held the opposing teams to scores of only nine, eight and six points. And between 1928 and 1938, Brigham's football teams won or tied for eight city championships.

The "Bulldogs." Their colors were purple and white, and their uniforms were covered with bright stars and memorable numbers. With his victories, Brigham helped to build a sustaining pride in this student body of whites, blacks, Chinese and Japanese. The spirit remains alive today—perhaps even more intense after surviving the severe racial tension of the 1970s.

Brigham, the man who looked like a dutiful office supervisor, displayed a flair for football coaching that was astonishing in its sophistication. He had the drillmaster's reverence for sound fundamentals, but he combined that quality with an almost poetic instinct for daring and improvisation. Make no mistake, he was a great football coach; his name surfaced every time there was a college opening, and Brig frequently augmented his limited high school income by coaching former college stars at the semi-pro level. He would have been a successful coach at any level of competition.

Clark Shaughnessy, a famous college coach of Brig's era, is practically bronzed in the college football annals because he first unveiled the colorful T-formation at Stanford, a formation now used by all professional teams. Brigham was using the T-formation before Stanford ever heard of Shaughnessy. He became the first to split off two wide receivers, a practice now common in more advanced arenas of football.

Garfield exploded on rival teams. They shifted, or they didn't shift when they were expected to shift. They were quick-hitting and highly disciplined. They ran "bootleg" plays and exciting "naked reverses," and they ran from the single wing and the double wing. Among Seattle sportswriters Brigham became known as "the sly fox of the East Side." And many years later, Johnny Cherberg, once a coaching rival of Brigham's at Cleveland High, then coach at the University of Washington, conceded, "Brig was far ahead of all of us in those years."

He had much more than just flair. His teams were soundly coached on defense and they moved in swift, attacking unison when they got the ball. More importantly, Brigham had the knack of drawing together Garfield's rich kids, poor kids, blacks and Asians, because he treated them as equals and drew out the best they had to give.

So out of those years came players like "Chuck" Carroll, who became an all-American back at Washington, and who later served for many years as King County prosecutor. There would be Jeff Heath, a fine running back, who later turned to baseball and became a star in the major leagues. There was Homer Harris, a crashing, pass-catching end, the first black player to captain a Big Ten team (at Iowa), who is now a dermatologist in Seattle. Brigham's track, football and basketball athletes included such as Fred Thieme, former vice-president at the University of Washington, later president at the University of Colorado; there was Frank Garretson, who rose to become a brigadier general in the United States Marines; there was the football player, Brennan King, who became the first black coach in the Seattle school system and in the state. And there were Phil Gai and the Brenner brothers, Charley and Bill, Seattle family names that any local resident will recognize when buying a loaf of bread today. Even as one records them, he knows that some fine figures will be unavoidably passed over. Brig's boys included such as Jack Sylvester, a local attorney and former state legislator; Pat Sutherland, a prosecuting attorney in Thurston County; Dr. Kenneth Olson, later chief of the diagnostic branch at the National Cancer Institute. And out of those years came the war heroes—Sammy Bruce, a talented Garfield running back, who became that rarity in World War II, a black bomber pilot. There were gifted Japanese athletes like Harry Yana-gimachi, Shiro Kashino, Mike Hirarhara, Sadao Baba and Eitaro Nakamura, who fought with the celebrated Nisei "Go For Broke" regiment in the Italian campaign. "What made Garfield so great was its unity," remembers Bert McNae, once a Brigham player, now a real estate figure in Seattle. "You see, it always was a 'stock pot' of ethnic diversity that somehow became a 'family' at Garfield High."

It is more than just a footnote to remember that a Garfield cheerleader and track man in the Brigham years was a tiny kid named Morrie Alhadeff, now head of Longacres racetrack. Out of this 'stock pot' come names like Bill Hosokawa, currently an editor at the *Denver Post* and author of such books as *The Two Worlds of Jimmy Yoshida* and *Thunder in the Rockies*. Artist Ted Rand once was editor of the *Garfield Messenger*.

Leon Brigham should be listed among those early midwest transplants to Seattle who became captivated by the Northwest outdoors. He climbed Mount Rainier at least sixty times during his active teaching years. It was Brigham and Harry Cunningham, a boys' advisor at Garfield, and Forrest (Bud) Greathouse of Lincoln, who established the early ski programs for Seattle high school students. By 1944, Leon Brigham had proved all there was to prove. He stepped aside as a Garfield coach and became the Seattle school system's first athletic director.

It can safely be said that no man in Seattle's history contributed more to Seattle's educational program, its athletic excellence, than Leon Brigham. He brought to administration the same innovative, precise gifts he applied to coaching. As athletic director, he brought Seattle schools into the State High School Athletic Association, and for the first time Seattle teams could compete for state championships. Brigham helped set in motion the building of Seattle's High School Memorial Stadium.

He brought night football games to Seattle; he helped set up the annual Thanksgiving Day game between Seattle's champion and the best team in the rest of the state. He made it possible for Seattle high school track teams to travel to state meets. He instituted the annual "football jamboree" at Memorial Stadium. He urged, even forced, the building of new, spacious gymnasiums, now fixtures at all Seattle schools. He pushed for and obtained four-man football coaching staffs, plus assistant coaches in baseball and basketball. He devised and implemented new ticket procedures to high school events and he created a central accounting system that saved Seattle schools hundreds of thousands of dollars. Leon Brigham retired in 1961, after forty years of service in the Seattle school system.

He left an enduring legacy, and nothing stopped at Garfield after he departed. In 1949, a strong-willed man, a long-time college referee, who later became Garfield's principal, turned out what is now remembered as Garfield's champion "all nationality team." The key six members of this basketball squad were Aaron Vederoff, a Russian; Mike McCutcheon, an Irishman; Ray Soo, a Chinese; Oscar Holden, a black, and two Jewish kids, Ray Moscatel and Don Ginsberg. "And if you want to add another note," says Frank Fidler, the team's coach, "then put it down that I am from the South."

After Brigham's departure would come John Boitano, who called himself "a disciple of Brig's." Boitano's teams, like Brigham's, showed flair and daring, using what Boitano calls "my garbage plays," but they were strong fundamentally and well-disciplined. Under Boitano, Garfield won three city titles and four Metro Division championships in his twelve years as coach. "It always was a melting pot," says Boitano, "every kind of kid you can think of. Garfield High always did have real leaders. There was a momentum of leadership when I came there, the kids responded to discipline, and I'm glad I could help the momentum along." Boitano recalls how "the whole neighborhood, mostly blacks, would turn out to watch our practices and cheer my garbage plays. The community support was strong, even for our second and third teams, because Garfield High was a focal point for the whole community."

And so it is today that Garfield goes on winning its share of athletic championships. Like many other racially mixed schools in America, Garfield went through troubled, even ugly times, in the late 1960s and early 1970s. Demonstrators milled in the streets outside the school; some readily walked inside the school to confront teachers and administrators.

Several white teachers transferred to other schools. Some of the white students, frightened by threats and hostility, also transferred out of Garfield. After serving a year and a half as principal, Frank Fidler went to the school administrators and suggested that he be replaced by a black principal.

In the years following those bitter, destructive times Garfield got itself back on track. Its football teams, not exactly reminiscent of the winning days of Brigham and Boitano, nonetheless won two Metro titles between 1977 and 1982. Its basketball teams excelled with two Metro titles, being state champions in 1980. And for the past three seasons, 1980 through 1982, Garfield's track teams, both boys and girls, have won the Metro title.

If athletics were all that make up Garfield, the school would be of no more than passing interest; but academically Garfield's students have done extremely well, even through the years of black revolt and protest. The school has turned out more than its share of National Merit finalists, twenty-five of them in the last ten years. Some 60 percent of Garfield students go on to college; 5 to 10 percent enter Ivy League or other eastern schools. In Scholastic Aptitude Tests, Garfield students have scored consistently higher than the mean average for the entire United States. A black principal, Ammon McWashington, presides over a student body that ranges in population from about 1,100 to 1,400. Its racial makeup, subdivided always in terms of ethnicity, comes out about roughly equal in number of blacks and whites, with smaller percentages of Asians, Filipinos, Hispanics and American Indians.

Garfield High today offers exemplary programs in science, math, and social studies. The school attracts students in marine biology and health sciences. The science program, begun at Garfield in 1977, was part of the school system's option programs to attract students from other districts to schools offering specialized areas of study. "But in all those years," says Boitano, reaching back into the 1950s, "anybody who went to Garfield and wanted good schooling could get it."

This superiority in science courses finds approximately 85 percent of the student body enrolled in science programs at Garfield—a staggering figure compared to other Seattle schools. Garfield now actively recruits students—especially minority students—for its science program. Science teacher Craig MacGowan gives evidence that Garfield's school spirit has not flagged when he says, "The parents go haywire when programs and teachers are cut—they don't hesitate to yell."

It is a long time since I first saw Charlie Russell run with a football at Hiawatha Playfield, or faced the stern countenance of Leon Brigham. Both of them have become my friends in the years since those first meetings. I see Charlie around town often. His skill as an athlete never was realized in college after he went to the university, but I have often thought that the school's racial climate, given the mentality of Washington coaches in that particular time of our history, did not augur well for a lone black kid, however gifted.

Last spring I drove down to Lacey, near Olympia, to find Leon Brigham again. During a long, pleasant afternoon we talked at great length about his glory days at Garfield High. Brig is eighty-six now, still a handsome, proud figure of a man, living in comfortable retirement with his wife, Clara. He unveiled a treasure trove of newspaper clippings, trophies and awards that came to him and his athletes at Garfield.

Many of his former players and students make the trek from Seattle to see him and his correspondence with them is brisk.

As we began to talk, Brig handed me a typewritten list (he had typed it himself) of people who had played for him. He had categorized them as "all-city or outstanding," "prominent citizens," "war heroes" and "team leaders." The list of seventy-seven bristled with a spectrum of names—Ted Isaacson, Sam Zedick, Harold Duffy, Ackie Kessler, Duke Hankinson, Bill Taylor, Leon Siegel, Vic Calderon, Ron Bekins, Bill Gasperetti, John Rupp, Al Franco, Eric Chew . . . on and on.

He flipped through one huge scrapbook until he came across a dramatic picture. This was an action photo of Harry Yanagimachi, the celebrated Japanese center he had in the 1930s, a boy so swift and strong that he, as the man who snapped the ball, could pull out of the line and lead interference. The photo showed the square-set figure of Yanagimachi lifting an opposing player off the ground on his broad shoulders, so perfectly was the block applied. "Now there," said Brig, proudly, "was a football player." He told of Charlie Russell, "a fine, sensitive kid, and a great, great runner," and Brennan King, "a great athlete," and of how Lieutenant Sammy Bruce, one of his favorite running backs, was killed on a bombing mission in Italy.

On that pleasant, full afternoon, Brig told of Al Franco, now a Seattle attorney, who was a small but determined guard on one of Garfield's basketball teams. Franco, as Brig told it, held a starting position on the varsity, but he tutored a taller, more gifted kid, in order to get him scholastically eligible for the team. "And Al did this," Brigham said, "knowing that if he got that taller guy eligible, the kid would replace him in the starting lineup."

He also told of Homer Harris, whose stature as a team leader never has been equaled at Garfield. Before Homer's senior year a ruling came down from the school board that players could no longer elect their team captains—the captain must be selected by the coach. "So I asked for a vote from the players, just to give me guidance in picking a captain," Brigham said. "The vote was from the whole squad, and I counted forty-seven pieces of paper. Every one of those slips had the name 'Homer Harris' on it—all except one. That was Homer's own. He wouldn't vote for himself."

One of Brigham's great players was his own son, Leon Brigham, Jr. who was nicknamed "Junie." He later went to Washington and Brigham recalled how Jimmy Phelan, the coach, called him aside before the Huskies took a trip to California. "He told me that Junie was the best end he had, but that if possible he wanted to hold him out of the California game and preserve another year of Junie's eligibility. They call it 'redshirting' these days. I said that was fine with me, and I looked forward to three seasons of watching Junie play end for Washington. But that summer Junie was killed on a climbing expedition near Mount Rainier."

Brigham was the man who couldn't sing when he was interviewed for his first job at Garfield High. He didn't have to. He coached its athletes to many titles and championships, and Garfield's musical heritage grew on its own. Its famous musical grads include such as Quincy Jones, who became a world class musician, arranger and record producer; Ernestine Anderson, Floyd Standifer and Buddy Catlett. Jimi Hendrix, the gifted rock musician who died at an early age, attended, but did not graduate from, Garfield. Garfield was one of the first schools in the area to institute a stage band program, back in the 1960s under the leadership of Waldo King. The program flourished for a while, faded, then evolved into what is now the Garfield Jazz Ensemble—a top drawer musical unit that has captured prizes three out of the last four years at the Reno Jazz Festival, largest festival of its kind in the nation for high school bands. The Garfield Ensemble placed No. 1 in the country the last two years.

The Ensemble itself typifies the diversity of Garfield. Half the group is white, half of it is black, or some other ethnic group. The ensemble of 1982 featured two piano players—David Reed, who is black, and Robin Reid, a girl, who is white. It was led by Garfield's musical director, Clarence Acox, who tells how audiences cracked up when his two piano players were introduced as "the Reed twins." "How can you get such a mix in players?" people ask him, and Acox's answer is definitive: "That's just Garfield High School—it's always like that."

It seems almost preordained that a kid like Yasser Seirawan would become a freshman at Garfield in 1975. Yasser was born in Damascus, of a Syrian father and an English mother. His skin is olive-dark, his eyes flash mischievously, and, barely into his teens out of Meany Middle School, his bold behavior and Afro hairdo made for an easy blend into Garfield's jivey mix. During his boyhood, growing up in Virginia Beach, Virginia, Yasser had been a pool hustler, a beach bum, a surfer, a snorkler and pinball shark. Now his bag was chess, a game he had discovered only a couple of years before he entered Garfield.

Yasser badgered Garfield officialdom to form a chess club. When it refused, he bootlegged his way into empty classrooms for practice and teaching sessions, rallying his buddies into forming their own school chess club. He demanded one hundred dollars for chess boards and chess clocks; he was turned down. Yasser's Garfield chess buddies were no less enthusiastic, and among them they fomented a student drive to raise the needed one hundred dollars. Mainly through the help of John Kunselman, a physics teacher, and James Stan, a teacher of art, the Garfield kids got going with their chess. That first year they were runners-up in Metro school chess competition. In 1976, they wiped out the Metro league, then won the regional high school championships in Yakima. Kunselman and Stan by this time were enthusiastic, and they transported the Garfield chess team to matches in their own cars, paying for their own gasoline. Chess trophies began to accumulate; Yasser, still very much the hustler, held them hostage from the school's trophy case until chess was granted "major sport" status. Then he demanded lettermen's jackets. On his own he went to Stan, the teacher of art, and said: "Design us a letterman's jacket. On it I want lots of stars, lots of stripes, a great big 'G' and the ugliest bulldog you can imagine right in the middle of it." Somehow he ramrodded this through, and to Yasser's delight, the first glimpse of Garfield's chess lettermen's jackets brought envious football and basketball players around saying, "Hey, man, how'd you get those cool jackets?"

In 1977, it was a repeat of past victories—the Metro title and the regional title. Now it was time for the nationals in Cleveland, Ohio. To get there, the six-person chess team needed eight thousand dollars. Witnesses to the Garfield spirit in action saw students, teachers, parents and friends rallying with car washes, candy sales and heavy lobbying with the school board to raise the money. Garfield finished second nationally, by a bare half-point, and the kid who lost the critical game was Yasser Seirawan. Yasser was glad it was he, and not one of his teammates, who had lost. Because by now Yasser had gained confidence, he had his eye on more prestigious tournaments, and the hurt of losing would have been harder on one of the others. He went to summer school that year, bypassed his senior eligibility, and went off to the chess wars.

On April 22, 1982, in the Greater London Council building, near Westminster Bridge and Big Ben, some of the world's foremost international chess grandmasters were gathered for the Philips & Drew Masters Chess Tournament. More than eight hundred chess aficionados, from Europe, Russia, and all over the world, watched the final match in the auditorium. On one side of the board sat Anatoly Karpov, a slight, sallow-faced, intent Russian, studying the placement of pawns, bishops, kings and queens over nearly four hours of play.

Karpov is a singular figure in world chess, a certified hero of the Soviet Union, where to millions of Russians, chess is what they have instead of religion. A notable Russian chess victory, or defeat by a foreigner, is felt strongly within the Kremlin itself. Karpov, as the reigning champion, has successfully defended his world title on two occasions; here, in London, he was the centerpiece of this invitational tournament, as he studied the board in a final match that would give him yet another tournament victory. Karpov surveyed the board morosely. He lost his composure only briefly, just long enough to glare at his second—then hit the clock to signify his surrender. He reached across the board and said to his opponent, "Congratulations on a good game."

"Thank you very much," replied the kid from Garfield High School as he accepted the resignation of the greatest chess player in the world.

12

Where is Home?

I have had more street addresses than a floating craps game, more forwarded letters than a shyster mail-order house, more phone numbers than a professional bookmaker, and enough paper boys to crowd a medium-sized junior high school. I can't think of a single place in Seattle that I don't care for; some places more than others, of course, but the urge to drift, to encounter new people, find new places and smell different neighborhoods, is a minor disease of the malignant type that afflicts sailors, hoboes and cockroaches.

Rainier Valley was a great place. For one thing, there was a beautiful ball park there once, but being a kid who personally did not know a single black, only one or two Japanese, and but a handful of Italians, the gamy "Garlic Gulch" of Rainier Valley was like visiting another nation. At Franklin High I got to know Italian kids like Ralph Yorio, Tony Maletta, George DiJulio, and a veritable dynasty of DiJulios since.

Ralph Yorio took me into his home once, and to this day I still can smell the rich odors of true Italian cooking, great chewy loaves of bread, homemade wine and strong cheeses, the first taste of which would make your eyes blink.

Out of this came a lifelong affection for Italians. I would come to know and love Victor Rosellini, a one-time waiter who became Seattle's peerless feeder of the expense account crowd. There would be Bill and John Gasperetti, who made the Roma Cafe a veritable city institution, where you could always drop in and find a retired halfback, a cop, perhaps the mayor, ready to talk and gossip. Bill Gasperetti epitomized what I see in most Italians—warm and effusive, each greeting loud and spontaneous, as though you had just returned after a long absence. Because I was drawn to Italian people, I came to care for Edo Vanni, Frank Sugia, Al Bianchi (the attorney, not the basketball coach), Vito and Jimmy Santoro, Johnny Greco and too many others to name.

Beacon Hill was just an interlude, but even as a high school kid I loved to shop in the Japanese stores along Beacon Ave., marveling at the mysterious sounds, a language I could never hope to understand, feeling delighted (and amazed) at the quiet behavior of little Japanese children, dark hair cut in straight bangs across their foreheads. Why is it, I wondered even then, you so rarely hear a Japanese child cry loudly in public?

I like to think—although it probably isn't true—that I lived on Beacon Hill at the same time George Tsutakawa ran a produce market on Jackson St. The cops arrested George and he was convicted in police court and fined five dollars by Judge William Devin (who later would be Seattle's mayor) for "obstructing the sidewalk" in front of his store with a display of merchandise. Many years passed before I got to know

George Tsutakawa, and if you have a faint notion you might have heard this name, Tsutakawa, get thee to the downtown public library to refresh your memory—by standing in front of the library's magnificent "Fountain of Wisdom." George built that fountain. It was his first—locally his most famous sculpture—one of many he would build in various cities of the world. Dedicated in 1960, it also was the first fountain to be erected in Seattle for more than twenty-five years; since then George has become a fountain sculptor of international repute. After the Fountain of Wisdom, Tsutakawa constructed seven other beautiful creations in Seattle and around the state, and he is, without question, one of our most distinguished citizens. He has done more for the city's quality than a hall full of badge-winners.

George is modest to a profound degree. He is resigned to the fact that he will not live long enough to do all the fountains he would like to do. "My job is that I am a craftsman," he told me one time. "If I do it well, it will last. And if somebody asks me to do a fountain, I will do my very best." When George's Fountain of Wisdom was ready to open in 1960, the pipes inexplicably sprung a large leak, and it was at this point—a true crisis—that he explained himself to the members of the Seattle Art Commission. He told them that building a fountain was like having a baby. "And a healthy baby," he said, grandly, "is designed to leak. The trouble we're having right now is that the diaper is leaking."

There is no record that Arts Commission members were reassured, but George plugged the leak, and he would later call it "my big gamble." He added: "It was a big gamble for everybody—and I was it. I knew that if I did this fountain right it would be the beginning of a fountain revival in Seattle. If I failed, there might be no more fountains in Seattle for another twenty-five years."

Why fountains? What's the importance of them? There was a time in Seattle when people asked questions like that, when "public art" was equated with wasting the money of taxpayers, and the mouth-breathers who ran the city then were, in the words of an old friend of mine, Tommy Brophy, "the kind of guys who would put clocks in the bellies of statues."

"Before I ever built fountains," George explained one time, "I used to build 'oboes.' These are little stone monuments the Tibetans build on mountain tops, sacred places and water sources. They honor the earth and point to heaven. My fountains are 'oboes' with the addition of a third element—moving water. Water is the most mysterious and elusive element in the natural world. It goes into the earth and up into the air. It can become vapor and it can become hard as stone. I don't know of anybody in the world who does not love water."

In retrospect, I always thought it would be a nice civic gesture if we could figure out some way for the city to give George back that five-buck fine he got for obstructing the sidewalk.

I lived quite a long time on Queen Anne Hill, first on the east side of it, then the west. Frankly, I never got a good handle on Queen Anne Hill, because when I lived there it was during senseless days of rushing about, putting down little dots to record hits and put-outs in a baseball scorebook; staying up too late, drinking too much, imparting too much emphasis on the wrong things. A few years ago, my friend, Dick Clever, then a reporter on the *P–I*, now with the *Times*, wrote the best story I ever saw on Queen Anne Hill. Dick did it with the imaginative device of catching the No. 2 bus at the end of the line and riding it downtown. His description is better than anything I can do on Queen Anne Hill. Hence, with gratitude:

West Queen Anne No. 2 lurches away from the curb near Mt. Pleasant Cemetery where lie the bones of many of the hill's pioneer citizens. No. 2's electric motor whines. The overhead transmission lines twang. The trackless trolley's big rubber tires swish on the rain-dampened street. It is 8:36 A.M.

The whine-twang-swish of the trolley mingles with the shouts of Queen Anne children running, skipping, roughhousing their way to school. And the route of the trolley is as predetermined as the parallel set of wires leading down the hill, as the quiet, staid, self-assurance of the solid, shoulder-to-shoulder pre-war homes that line the hilltop streets.

Running along Sixth Ave., the No. 2 will stop and take on her cargo of passengers for downtown. Many are young men, in their 20s and 30s, dark-suited, some wearing legal pinstripes, lugging briefcases. They sit in sober contemplation, watching the blur of houses whip by the window. Then, near the southern ridge of the hill, come the elderly and retired people who emerge from the doughty old brick apartment houses. They struggle to mount the steps of the electric bus.

Then, as No. 2 descends the slopes of Queen Anne Ave. with her driver tapping a rhythmic dance on the brake pedal, come the young women from their efficiency apartments. Career women, secretaries, stenographers for the downtown offices and brokerage houses. They come with cheeks flushed red from the brisk morning chill. They wear long, stylish coats, bright knitted hats, swatches of color upon their lips, neatly penciled brows. The sweet aura of perfume begins to permeate No. 2.

Just as the aroma is becoming maddening to the young men with their briefcases, No. 2 begins disgorging her passengers along First Ave. The dwellers of the hill begin their day. It is a pattern repeated through the seasons. It is the quiet rhythmic obbligato of the hill. Other neighborhoods were slashed and torn by the juggernaut of economic decline and fall, of orgiastic high construction and suburbanization. Not Queen Anne.

The old lady did survive it all. Queen Anne is little different from the days when my two daughters went to John Hay and Coe schools, and later Queen Anne High, now closed forever. What Dick Clever called "Seattle's in-town bedroom" has remained pretty much the same. The "counterbalance," so named for the underground counterweights, which helped get the old trolleys up the still formidable avenue that rises to the top of Queen Anne, is long gone. But the views remain. The development of Seattle Center inevitably attracted the developers, thirsting and gaping, full of ideas for throwing up huge view-blockers on the south slope. But a doughty group of Queen Anne residents, banded into something called United South Slope Residents, fought them off. Their subversive-sounding acronym, USSR, made for an amusing irony, since Queen Anne Hill long has been known as rock-solid Republican.

Through most of the 1950s and part of the 1960s, I lived with my wife, Betty, and two daughters, Lea Ann and Nancy, on the west side of the hill overlooking Pier 91 and Elliott Bay. Betty is a marvelous woman, tall and vivacious, and she made our big old barn of a house into a veritable clubhouse for neighborhood kids and friends. The rear of the house was on West View Drive, a curving street that had almost a European flavor, and on occasion, across the street, a well-known Seattle chef named "Papa Jack" Karamanos, would roast a whole lamb on a barbecue spit he constructed in his back yard. The roasting would begin early in the morning, and by noon the aroma was enough to drive one into a frenzy. By mid-afternoon, Greek relatives and friends descended on the neighborhood, and the feast lasted far into the evening, followed by Greek folk dancing in the Karamanos' basement.

Because I was too full of myself, doing "important things" like putting more dots in more scorebooks, Betty raised the girls. They grew up tall and strong and very beautiful; they are endowed with their mother's vivaciousness, her readiness to accept all people on their own terms, and to count the least among her acquaintances as equal on any scale of alleged importance. They are wonderful.

Just as you break over the brow of the counterbalance there is an old Victorian house, the occupants of which had a distinct effect on much of what I did. These were the Donohoes. It would be the second time in my life when I would be exposed to the wild, almost anarchic nature of a large Irish Catholic family. I never did learn how many Donohoes there are; eight, I think. I got to know Madeline quite well; she was an outstanding tennis player, a strong and forceful woman, who is now married to Lenny Anderson, a gifted writer with whom I traveled thousands of miles on the baseball beat. And there was Mike. Mike was the oldest. He had a sharp, sardonic wit and together, before he gave the game back to the boys, we drank rivers of Scotch in the old

Italian Club on Union Street. In significant ways, Mike was the wisest of us all, a man with enviable "street smarts," and a worldly knowledge of fraud and chicanery, formed out of the Depression years and many summers of covering the racetrack at Longacres.

If Queen Anne Hill never produced anything else, it could rest on its laurels (perhaps with a troubled conscience) when it gave the city Ed Donohoe. Even his brother Mike, the most worldly of men, could only shake his head at the wonder of his younger brother, Edmund. It is useless to estimate how many sacred cows Ed Donohoe has attacked—and in varying degrees deflated—with his diatribes in the *Washington Teamster*. Most "house organs," be they corporate or union, are unfit for the bottoms of bird cages, being soporific, self-congratulatory and so censored as to be beyond redemption. Not the *Washington Teamster*. Regularly, a ritual occurs at the Teamsters headquarters, a rambling, one-story brick building at Taylor and Denny. Arnie Weinmeister, the over-all boss of the Western Conference of Teamsters and Ed Donohoe's ultimate editor, finishes reading Donohoe's next column. "He doesn't censor me," says Ed, proudly. "He says he just wants to read it first so he'll know where the beefs will come from."

I first met Ed Donohoe when he was a skinny, hunched-over scholar at St. Martin's College in Lacey, where he earned his keep as a "publicity director" for this august institution. His employer was the legendary football player, Joe Paglia, who in those days coached the school's football team, its basketball team and its baseball team, sweeping out the gym and keeping Donohoe out of trouble in his spare time. He had hired Ed as his "publicity director" when Ed was only a student, the job paying out with board, room and tuition for his manly labors. "You don't get free books because you aren't worth it," Paglia told him.

Donohoe put St. Martin's athletic teams before the public in ways that not even Paglia could foresee. He fed the local press (and wire services) stories about Paglia's "feud" with some rival coach; he delighted sports scribes with wild, sometimes fabricated, stories about Paglia's trick plays, or some new (perhaps non-existent) superstar, and the devilish fate that awaited such opponents as Pacific Lutheran and College of Puget Sound. "Good Lord," I heard Paglia exclaim once, "that stuff was so wild it was embarrassing to walk down the streets of Olympia." Donohoe, to every newsie's profound regret, finally lost his job. This came about partly because he talked up a plan to recruit a well-known Tacoma prostitute as St. Martin's "homecoming queen."

Ed Donohoe went off to the South Pacific in World War II, where he served in the medical corps, advancing the cause of democracy as a "bedpan commando"—his own term—in America's crusade to liberate the Free World from Japanese aggression. With the 81st Division he got a Bronze Star for bringing out wounded buddies under fire. Returning to the civilian combat theatre, he almost blew his first big job with the Teamsters Union, then ruled by Dave Beck. The union's powerful leader, a veritable volcano of ideas, concocted a plan to build "hitchhiking shelters" for service men. Donohoe was ordered to establish a beachhead on the unfriendly shores of the *Seattle Times*, never an admirer of Beck's or of any other union. "Get out of here," a *Times* editor told Donohoe. "We know what you bastards are up to." Donohoe shrugged his skinny shoulders and returned with his report to Beck. "They threw me out," he told Beck. "The editor said he knows what you bastards are up to." Donohoe escaped unemployment, but he never was close to Beck after that.

In his thirty-two years of being Seattle's best-known curmudgeon, Donohoe has lambasted an amazing array of citizens and professions. He has erupted in seeming frenzy against nurses, doctors, lawyers, judges, prosecutors, television announcers and various innocent bystanders, whose only crime seemed to be an acquaintance with the object of Donohoe's vitriol. Ed Donohoe, as devout a Catholic as you will find this side of the Vatican, once excoriated the late Cardinal Spellman in, of all things, His Eminence's obituary notice. Ed remembered that Cardinal Spellman once tried to break a gravediggers' strike.

He continues to lash out at the *Times* ("Fairview Fanny") and the League of Women Voters ("a henhouse of leather-skinned busybodies"). If everybody loved the Pike Place Market, Ed found it to be "a rat-infested place for winos" and suggested we do away with the whole thing. He gave enduring, scathing nicknames to people. Charles Carroll, the former city councilman, was known forever as "Streetcar Charlie," because Carroll had once been a trolley conductor. Lud Kramer, once Washington's Secretary of State, was tagged as "Lud the Dud," when he served on Seattle's city council. The former King County prosecutor, Chuck Carroll, a legendary football All-American at the University of Washington, became "Fair Catch" Carroll, and he once referred to an old drinking buddy of his, namely me, as "a limp-wristed liberal." In his drinking days, Ed was a menace to society. When duly snockered, he had a compulsion to shriek loud insults in bars. He could fall down stairs with the best of them and when driving he developed the unbreakable habit of ignoring stop signs.

Faced with a blizzard of DWI charges, Ed bowed to the

inevitable. "Letting me drive a big car was like putting an idiot in a Sherman tank." So he sold the car, quit drinking, and enrolled at the University of Washington, where he finished his schooling only ten hours short of a bachelor's degree in English. This latter fact never ceases to amaze readers of his column, who number more than fifty thousand.

Noting his high readership, the *P-I* went slightly off its rocker one day by hiring Ed Donohoe to write a weekly column. What it didn't reckon was this: it is one thing to blithely insult all segments of a community in the relatively small circulation vortex of the *Washington Teamster*, a journal free of advertisers. Moreover, *Teamster* readers had become conditioned to Donohoe's Mencken-like flailing. It is quite another thing, however, to let Donohoe loose on the un-suspecting subscribers of a general circulation newspaper.

Before long, he had the *P-I*'s libel attorneys reaching for tranquilizers. At one point, a peace-making luncheon was arranged by the publisher, Dan Starr, between Donohoe and the late Paul Ashley. The latter was a pillar of the local estab-lishment, properly cautious and conservative, and a man who had authored a local treatise on libel called *Say It Safely*. This luncheon-style effort to establish detente began to grow shaky before the salad arrived. It broke down completely during the soup course. Instead of being contrite, Donohoe attacked Ashley with a frontal assault. "I hear you're writing a sequel to that book," he said contemptuously, of Ashley's biblical work on libel. "You're gonna call it *Leave It Out*. For Crissakes, you wouldn't let a guy print the Ten Command-ments!"

So Edmund, the Fearless Journalist, went back to souring milk among Seattle's sacred cows, in the *Washington Teamster*.

Ed and I still have lunch together, and I treasure those days when the phone rings and his low, rasping voice comes on the line, "Hey, did you see what that son of a bitch did? You know who I mean. Why, I'll—" We need guys like Ed. The city is too monochromatic.

The No. 2 Queen Anne bus doesn't pass the house of Edo Vanni, but if I were in the tour bus business I would route it past this Seattle landmark. Down at Seattle Center, when you come in the south entrance, you wind past the fun zone and up where the Steig kids bounce balls against the Horiuchi mural. If you turn left and walk a ways you will arrive about where the old Warren Ave. grade school used to stand. The school produced a fairly tough brand of kids, including Edo Vanni. Actually, Edo was raised more or less in Black Diamond, where they played a lot of soccer, and when Edo Vanni hit Queen Anne High, he already was a better drop-kicker and place-kicker than most of our institutions of higher learning were able to graduate. Edo played football and the University of Washington gave him a scholarship just to kick field goals and try-for-points. That was an ill-starred conception, because a place-kicker, for the most part, is a fairly passive observer, and Edo is about as passive as a truant when the circus is in town.

I said I liked Italians. Well, I came to love Edo, although it didn't start out that way. I played baseball against him, and you don't easily become fond of a guy who can figure out eight ways to beat you and all of them embarrassing. He came down off Queen Anne Hill like a cyclone, owning the strongest tonsils and the largest nose in local baseball culture. He got out of the University of Washington before he made the mistake of cracking his first book. He signed on with the old Seattle Rainiers, just as they moved into their new digs at Sicks'

Stadium in 1938. Edo added his lustre to that dedication. He registered the first base hit ever recorded there, he stole the first base in Sicks' Stadium, and he scored the new park's first run.

And when they closed it thirty years later for extensive renovation before Seattle's first try at major league baseball, they had a special "Edo Vanni Night." As well they might have.

Edo, you see, has always been a special part of Seattle. When he signed on with the Rainiers out of high school, he got a $3,500 bonus. Most kids from a poor background would have headed for the nearest clothing store or car dealer. The first thing Edo did with all that money was to buy a house for his mother and father. Then he went on a rampage. He hit .330 in his first year of professional ball; he stole bases, he shagged flies, he talked a blue streak, and old "banana nose" became a fourteen-carat sports hero, not only to the Italians in Seattle, but to everyone else.

He had some brilliant seasons before World War II, but after that some of the old skills slipped away. He suffered a badly broken leg with Seattle in 1946, and eventually he ended up in what was then known as the Western International League. But he didn't leave without a struggle, finishing out his Seattle career in 1950. His leave-taking was as memorable as his entrance. As an old player—his last game, in fact—he sat on the Seattle bench and gloomily watched his team lose, a team he had once sparked to three straight championships. As Vanni watched, a veritable cascade of home runs—five in all—sailed over the fence against Seattle pitching that can only be described as horrible. "Vanni," ordered his manager, "get in there and play left field."

Edo reached for his glove which hung on a hook in the dugout. Just as he started out on the field he turned and said, "Which side of the fence?"

So he went to the lower minors, and in cities like Wenatchee, Spokane, Yakima and elsewhere, they remember him to this day. He was a player, then a playing manager, and finally just a manager. In those days he nurtured dozens of young players, teaching them his wiles and skills, sending them on to the major leagues, trying to impart his own message—win, win, win . . . the world is full of losers . . . be a winner! And in those days, he laid down a sensible credo of conduct.

"Kiddies," he would tell them, "you take care of the baseball and old Dad will take care of the drinking."

The game of baseball gave Edo a lot. He used his money wisely, built up security for himself and his family; it is no business of mine to guess his net worth today, but it is considerable. And if baseball helped to give him all this, Vanni paid baseball back in kind. When he left it, he didn't owe the game a thing. For all through his career he did his best to promote attendance, to arouse interest, to rescue the world—his part of it—from the humdrum.

He never fined a player for fighting on the field. A player was fined only if he was the last one to enter a fight. He once stimulated five fights simultaneously on the field and was fined fifty dollars for it. "So it cost me ten dollars a fight," he explained later, "but the next night people broke down the turnstiles to see us play. At ten dollars a fight, I figure that was a bargain for the franchise."

To draw fans into the park, he once wrestled a bear before a game in Salem, Oregon. In order to arouse the fans and spark attendance in Edmonton, he raged against an umpire's decision, then climbed the grandstand's protective screen, like a monkey, to further dramatize the perfidy he was forced to endure. He got entangled in the screen and it took an emergency call to the Edmonton fire department to get him down so the game could go on. And once, when he kicked a board out of the dugout in frustration, he was presented a bill for twenty-five dollars from the home team for repairs. To express his disgust, he went out and bought some lumber and fashioned his own dugout for the next night's game.

He once ran for the state legislature as a Democrat "because I wanted to stir things up." During the campaign he noticed a large number of cars, belonging to enemy Republicans, parked near the apartment building he owns on lower Queen Anne. They were attending a GOP rally at the old Civic Auditorium. Edo brooded over his opportunity for only a minute, then went into action. Two hours later, hundreds of cars, driven by unsuspecting Republicans, left their political assignation ablaze with unnoticed bumper stickers: "Vanni For State Rep."

One year in the 1960s—I forget which year; it doesn't matter now—Edo became manager of the Seattle Rainiers. It was an appointment long overdue. Given some of the stumblebums they had hired before him, Edo returned like a breath of fresh air. It was most fitting, it seemed to me, that the kid who once got the first hit in Sicks' Stadium would finally become the boss in that same stadium.

We spent the afternoon together celebrating his appointment. I took time off from work and we roamed around the city; suddenly we found ourselves at Woodland Park, for what reason I cannot remember and don't care to. We wandered into the ape house to study our esteemed cousin, the late great Bobo, a gorilla of impressive dimensions. I asked Edo if he felt at all overwhelmed at being the new manager of the Rainiers.

He said no, not especially. "But I was just thinking, I need a blaster to hit clean-up for me. I wish I could draft that ape."

Counting up the neighborhoods where I lived starts out as fun, then ends up faintly embarrassing. There was West Seattle, of course, then Beacon Hill, then Rainier Valley and the warm richness of Garlic Gulch; a brief period in the U District, then Rainier Beach, Queen Anne, West Seattle again, then Capitol Hill for a while, a place on the lake at Leschi, then Madison Park. I'm glad I lived in Madison Park once, because that kind of completes the circle; it was a move that subtly told me something about myself and the city I love.

Madison Park is old Seattle, a romantic part of the city that dates back to an age when the trip out there was a considerable journey, where Seattleites went to spend their vacations. There used to be a race track in Madison Park, and most of the houses along 41st and 42nd Aves. are small, being one-time "beach houses" made over and renovated into permanent homes. It is almost an axiom that if you start from the mansions of Washington Park and move east toward Lake Washington, the number of bedrooms gradually declines.

Madison Park is quite glossy now (some of the lake condos sell for breathtaking prices) but it still somehow retains the flavor of a resort community. Unofficially, it begins at McGilvra Blvd. and ends at the foot of Madison St. where the remnant of a ferry dock still stands, a dock that once berthed ferries which traveled to Medina, Hunts Point and Kirkland.

The Madison Park Bakery still is a place for morning pastry, coffee, gossip and small talk, and a pleasant array of shops lines the north side of the street. But the focal point of Madison Park, its tiny Pentagon for housing, ordinance, supplies and information, is the Madison Park Hardware store. No place quite like it exists in all of Seattle. It is run by a

remarkable couple, Lola and Bud McKee, especially Lola, a
woman of formidable intelligence, independence and compassion.

You need a dentist? Lola will find you a dentist, even on
weekends. You need a job? Lola knows where a job has just
opened up. If your need is a psychiatrist, she will steer you to
the right head-shrinker. A recipe for coffee cake? She's got
that, too. Madison Park Hardware's bulletin board is a
kaleidoscope of cards, memos and personal messages; there
are "work needed" notices and "help wanted" signs. There
are signs to advertise church socials, political meetings, or
caucuses to promote causes. Even if she doesn't like your
politics or your cause, Lola gives you space to advertise your
aberration. Want a baby-sitter? Check with Lola. Need an
apartment? Lola knows when one is opening up.

The McKees' hardware store is an incredible, gloriously
cluttered cornucopia of practical items—from the smallest
Phillips screwdriver to the finest in gourmet cookware.
Whole generations of young people have learned from Lola
and Bud, and from their now-retired assistant, Glenn Fain—
how to fix a leaky faucet, how to trap a rat in the basement,
what kind of paint to use, how to seal a window, ad
infinitum. In our Saran-wrapped age of computers and
checkout counters, Madison Park Hardware is a reassuring
bastion of human intercourse, friendship and trust. This tiny
store, incredibly, carries more than eight hundred private
charge accounts.

There are many stories, never verified because the McKees
do not talk about it, of money slipped to needy students, of
hundreds of small, private kindnesses that emanate from their
remarkable hardware store. It is said, perhaps apocryphally,
that Lola has three prices: 10 percent off to people she really

likes, 10 percent off to people who pay their bills within thirty days, and yet another, higher price for people she doesn't know well, or knows too well to like them. Whatever, she is fond of saying, "God didn't let me pick my relatives, but I can pick my own friends."

A trained sociologist, it seems to me, could have a lot of fun investigating Madison Park. A lot of Madison Park residents are born in Washington Park, a few blocks up the hill. They go to Bush School, then to the University of Washington, if not some Ivy League school. Once out of college, they move into Lake Court, a bungalow-apartment complex on the lake that has housed the progeny of some of Seattle's more prominent families. They join Junior Club and the women, as in a rite of baptism, are inducted into the Junior League and Children's Orthopedic Hospital guilds. By now they are married, move into nearby Edgewater, and in due course they wheel baby carriages into the Madison Park Bakery. When success comes, as it inevitably does to people like this, they move back to Washington Park or into Broadmoor. They keep a charge account at the IGA and almost certainly maintain membership in the Tennis Club. And finally, when the time comes, they move into Park Shore, the luxury retirement home in Madison Park.

It was a happy interlude, Madison Park, but I became vaguely unsettled there. Perhaps it happened once too often, walking past the pharmacy toward the lake on a Saturday morning, and seeing one too many of the bright young men, upwardly mobile—very upward, very mobile—wearing their forty dollar turtleneck sweaters, leaning on their Mercedes 280 SL's. Once too often, perhaps, seeing the women, fresh in from the Tennis Club in their bright, expensive outfits, carrying racquets that cost ninety-five dollars, well-tanned, a bit too well-tanned, irritatingly sure of themselves, viewing the world with that special confidence that comes only from a comfort zone protected by prosperous insularity. It was all too homogenized.

Since then, for the most part, I have lived close to downtown, the real core of the city; for a while I lived in the Pike Place Market, more recently in the Denny Regrade. Increasingly, the inner city is becoming more alive, more varied; the Regrade is developing a neighborhood character of its own. It still lacks the cohesion of a real neighborhood, but one can readily find a sort of small-town camaraderie, easy acquaintances, comfortable distances, a striking diversity of people and places in the heart of the city itself. This, it seems to me, is real progress.

13

No Sad Songs

The Remlinger U-Pick berry farm, near Carnation, is a lovely, neatly-planted piece of ground with long rows of strawberry plants, carefully weeded and a delight to the picker. These acres of strawberry plants were once partly wooded with mostly alder trees and thick underbrush; some of these acres used to be covered by the oats my father grew there to feed our horses and three milk cows; yet another part was where we grew peas to sell and had the family vegetable garden. I once roamed these acres with a dog I named "Husky." Sometimes I played the big hunter with a BB gun, or carried an alder staff, acting out the role of Little John in *The Merry Tales of Robin Hood*. I sometimes go back there to pick strawberries. And it occurs here, willy-nilly, that picking strawberries is much like writing a book.

That is, you stoop along, taking the easy berries, sometimes popping one into your mouth, filling the basket. When you return and inspect the row you have just picked, there under the leaves, overlooked the first time, are the good berries you missed. In retracing your steps you find that you have picked too quickly, perhaps too carelessly, but time has run out and it is growing late. The guillotine awaits, and all editors descend from Madame LaFarge.

So much more to tell. I'm sorry that I didn't tell you more about a man I once loved, Fred Hutchinson, a childhood friend with a strange, indefinable, strain of greatness in him. He was a baseball manager—no more, no less—but he had the gift of rallying people to him, of making them perform up to his own fierce, exacting standards. You will go quite a distance and stay quite a while, in corporate board rooms or in Congress, to find a leader as good as he was. He died at a tragically young age, at peak of his powers, and even at this distance I find it painful to write about him.

There should have been more in this book about Victor Rosellini; not a chronicle of his skill at running a restaurant, but about the hundreds of small things he did to make Seattle better. I should have told you something of "Pop" Reed, a coach I once knew, whose interest in kids went far beyond what they could do with a bat and a ball, whose rhythm of speech, gift for simile and metaphor, sharpened my interest in writing. He coached far better than he knew.

This tome should have had something in it about Bill Baillargeon, a banker, who chose not to build another monstrous high-rise, but instead gave Seattle a small, human-scale center of respite on an otherwise drab part of lower Third Ave. The fault lies here for not including, among the city's Establishmentarians, the name of Bagley Wright who, more than anyone else, gave us the Seattle Repertory Theatre.

There should have been an attempt to capture the meaning

of John Goldmark, his life, his standards, his belief in excellence. John Goldmark, my friend, was born, bred and educated in the East, but he enriched this region and city by his presence. He was as close to being a Renaissance man as Seattle has ever seen—a rancher and lawyer, a master of language, a superb pilot, a pragmatic intellectual, and a formidable force in the state legislature. Red Smith said one time, "Dying is no big deal. The least of us can manage that. Living is the trick." John Goldmark died bravely against a background of pain and despair that would have crushed a lesser man. Yet it always seemed to me that he gave death the dispassionate contempt it deserves, a detail to be left waiting while the more important trick of living was mastered. As nearly as anyone I know, John mastered it, and I should have tried to tell you how.

Other stories, some sad, some funny, were regrettably left out. I never got anything in here about Dick Sharp, the boxing writer, who devised a scheme for making his own soap to sell during World War II when there was a shortage of soap. He was a good boxing writer, but a failure at making soap, which he brewed in the trunk of his car. You could smell him for blocks as he drove to work. I didn't recount the story of Bob Wark, an itinerant boxing manager, who walked away from nineteen plane crashes and once crash-landed his tiny one-seater on the roof of the old Bon Marche. I also should have worked in the story of a rangy young kid at Seattle University who was trying to make the basketball team.

His coach, Horace Albert Brightman, had decreed that none of his players could risk the team's welfare by going skiing. This kid broke the rule by going to Stevens Pass. On his way home a car in front of him skidded off the road, rolling over a bank into a snow-covered ditch. Much was made in the papers the next day about how the kid jumped down the bank to rescue the occupants of the car. Horace Albert Brightman, whatever his other shortcomings, could read. He summoned the young man into his office, showed him the newspaper and said, "You'd rather go play on mountains? Go play on mountains. You're off the team."

Nine years later, on May 1, 1963, the young man stood at the top of another mountain in the Himalayas—and the world soon learned that Jim Whittaker was the first American ever to climb Mount Everest.

If these pages seemed to dwell too much on the Great Depression it is because this American catastrophe had a profound effect on me, just as it did on millions of others, in my formative years. I did not suffer immensely from the Depression because my mother and father, two older brothers and two older sisters, did what they could to shield me from its ravages. But no kid, aware of the commissary lines, the public works, the loss of pride among fellow humans, could come out of it unscathed.

John Kenneth Galbraith, the economist, has written extensively about the great crash of 1929 which plummeted everyone, including my family, into bewilderment and despair. 'The Great Depression," he has written, "left no part of the nation and very few individuals untouched. Workingmen became unemployed or lived in fear that they would. There was no unemployment compensation on which they could expect to land. Farmers went bankrupt or feared they would. Nor was there anyone to whom they could hope to turn. Economic misfortune had a hopeless terminal quality in those days. And even in the depression the unemployed worker and the broken farmer could not entirely escape the ethos, some of it the residue of social Darwinism, that unemployment or bankruptcy marked a man as an inferior being.''

To this day, no matter how well things have gone with jobs on newspapers, I have never lost the tiny touch of fear that I might soon be out of work. Sometimes on trips I would wake up in the middle of the night, sweating, from a nightmare in which I had forgotten to file a story or had committed some ghastly blunder that would get me fired. If I cling to athletics too much in this narrative, it is because athletics—baseball, at least—meant a job when jobs were hard to get. You dreamed of playing professional baseball not only because it seemed glamorous, you played it because—hell, it meant a job. You played for a company-sponsored team because you could get employment from it. In reviewing my less than luminous struggle with the work ethic, every job I ever had came directly, or indirectly, from the fact of once having played baseball. So I worked at Todd Shipyards, Seattle-Tacoma Shipyards, Kirkland Shipyards, Longacres, Boeing, out of the Longshoremen's Hall, as a playfield instructor for the Seattle Parks Department, in the fruit orchards of Chelan, for an oil company in Billings, Montana, swamping packages for the May Company in Los Angeles and for Frederick & Nelson in Seattle—all because of baseball. Even a ham-and-egger like me could use his limited talent to work the right ''connection,'' to get the most menial of jobs. If none of you ever had to do any of this, rest assured—you didn't miss a thing.

''When the end of the world comes, Seattle will have one more year,'' a saying has it. I used to think that was true, but not any more. The rush of events has caught up with us; the Cascades no longer protect us from ''those easterners''; the technology of Boeing has drawn us uncomfortably closer to the nation and the rest of the world. What the sociologists call "in-migration" has affected us in ways we still do not comprehend, and a city once almost lily white now accommodates many ethnic varieties—Vietnamese, Cambodians, Chicanos, and more Japanese, more blacks. This is good.

We were once insular, even smug, content in our remoteness, and our politicians, instructed by the business interests which helped to elect them, turned sluggish inaction into an art form. But underlying this civic contentment was the disturbed feeling that we were somehow lacking as a city, as a place of variety, culture, color and awareness. This gave rise, I think, to repeated schemes to "put Seattle on the map." Not many people realize it today, but our summer festival known as Seafair was launched with a strong commercial impetus; behind it was the often stated goal—to get Seattle "the national recognition it deserves." So we did looney things. We accepted a spurious overlay of "commodores," and "admirals" and "Neptunes" and "pirates," and we even conducted public drives for money to help millionaires run their hydroplanes on Lake Washington. No real harm was done, and we came out of it with a pleasant summer diversion. But such nonsense, if proposed in these less innocent times, would get hooted out of town.

The World's Fair itself was another "put Seattle on the map" venture, and again, it was one that turned out well. We were lucky. Probably the World's Fair was a turning point in the city's growth; it did bring new people, new ideas into the city. But I remember, with perverse amusement, that the urbane *Manchester Guardian* correspondent, Alistair Cooke, paid us a visit. Cooke wrote a scalding critique of the fair, over what he called its "blatant commercialism" and he described, most accurately, the view of Seattle from the Space Needle, a view of naked, treeless streets and endless parking lots. The defensive uproar was glorious.

The World's Fair—or maybe it was just circumstances of the time—began drawing new, gifted, more progressive people to Seattle. If you say the growth of Boeing helped, you may have a point; but anyone who wishes to plumb the depths of urban awareness among Boeing engineers had best hunt his specimens in Split-Levelsville, far from the real concerns of a city. The kinds of people I noticed came from the East; they were young, well-educated, active; they were eager to live in Seattle's neighborhoods and work to make the city better. I used to call them the "Harvard Mafia," a loose nickname meant in jest. And gradually, in the 1960s, their presence began to be felt. Many came here to teach, men like Roger Sale, a writer and scholar of surpassing excellence, who authored a fine book, *Seattle, Past and Present.*

In the mid-1960s, Stimson Bullitt founded *Seattle* magazine, a publication that may have been ahead of its time in this city. But the magazine, edited by Peter Bunzel, a confirmed easterner, began to question, even attack, many of our contented assumptions. Stimson Bullitt's ill-fated brainchild, though it lasted little more than six years, attracted gifted writers like Charles Michener, Barry Head and David Brewster.

The *Weekly*, later founded by Brewster, became a delayed, foster offspring of *Seattle* magazine. At first erratic and a bit precious, the *Weekly* has become a commercially profitable news magazine with less of *Seattle*'s earlier slickness; it manages to convey a feeling that its own skepticism is firmly grounded in a genuine concern for the city's advancement. The *Weekly* adds a needed dimension to local journalism.

Like Bunzel, Brewster gathered around him some first-rate writer-reporters, many of whom, like Roger Downey, Cynthia Wilson and Fred Brack, are relatively new to Seattle.

These relative newcomers from the East, the Midwest and elsewhere, found in Seattle a place still young and beautiful enough to be saved from the horrors that afflicted many other American cities. Bright, earnest and well-educated, they not only got into communications, politics and education, they also emerged in the arts, in law, and in public action groups.

Something like intellectual guerrillas, they helped to bring down what *Seattle* once called "our musty, crusty" power structure. They combined with the region's own young progressives in a force that still is felt today. Thus it was that CHECC (Choose an Effective City Council), a cadre well-represented by eastern immigrants, helped elect Tim Hill and Phyllis Lamphere to the City Council in 1967. Later would come John Miller and Bruce Chapman. Chapman is gone, but Miller, after trying unsuccessfully for higher office, is now a commentator on public affairs for KIRO television and radio. Indeed, it was a former KING television commentator, Charles Royer, an "outsider" from Oregon City, Oregon, who became the city's mayor in 1978.

A relative newcomer, Paul Schell, became one of the most creative bureaucrats in the city's history as head of the city's Department of Community Development. Beaten by Royer in the race for mayor, Schell now guides a development firm devoted to restoration and the revival of fine old Seattle buildings. Attorney Llewelyn Pritchard has served as president of the Seattle Symphony, and his counterparts can be found everywhere, often siding with and supporting such enlightened local activists as Victor Steinbrueck, Ibsen Nelsen and Fred Bassetti.

Starting in the 1960s and continuing in the 1970s, more progressive forces began to shape the city. Many are local, but their ranks are spiced by "outsiders," the kind once viewed with suspicion in Seattle. In large measure they rallied behind a young and unknown Seattle engineer, Dan Evans, who served for twelve years as the best governor this state ever had. We were lucky.

A man I admire once said that he had a simple test in examining the worth of a city. He wrote, "It is whether, no matter how many times I have been there, I still feel a glow of excitement on the moment of arrival." I cannot speak for anyone else in thinking of Seattle this way, but whenever I leave it for any period of time, the glow is always there when I return. It is a beautiful city, unbelievably blessed by nature, but the late Seattle artist, Mark Tobey was right when he said, "It isn't always the place, you know." It's the people in a city, and this book has been about some of them.

I'm not sure if the change is in me or in Seattle itself. But it used to be that I was somehow faintly apologetic about "being from Seattle," possibly because I detected a subtle condescension in distant places about my city. In those days I looked with envy on Chicago, Denver, Los Angeles, New York—I tried to land jobs in all of those cities—because I saw them as places with more substance and excitement. If such a view was probably wrong then, it is certainly wrong now. Define substance, define excitement; they are in the eye of the beholder. But on the off-chance that anyone thinks the way I once did, I beseech him to give pause. Pause and reflect how lucky we are, how good we have made it, how easy it is to live here, how much better it can be. And if someone asks you about Seattle and in any way you feel compelled to "be" something to justify living here, play it as it lays.

Be delighted, my friend; be delighted.

What are chances? What are the "projections," as they say over mystic numbers and curving lines, that make up a graph of the future? If that is the question, you have come to the wrong writer. I can only suggest what I think a city should be, how it should grow and function, the way it should develop and flourish.

A city should be above all else diverse. It should instantly divest itself of any notion, a notion many in Seattle still have, that we can escape the discomfort of change. Many have tried with a flight to the suburbs; it doesn't work. A city should accommodate, willingly, all points of view, and not ever be suckered by incantations using the slippery catchword, "progress," spelled with a capital "P." Progress, made carefully, has its place. It should not be the mindless catch-all for narrow interests. A city is too important to turn itself over solely to commercial interests; a city should have too much pride to let itself become what a few bottom-line rubes in polyester suits want it to be.

Using a perhaps strained analogy, a city should be like the old stew pot bubbling on the stove in less prosperous times; a kettle of nourishment, host to variety, always simmering, subtly changing flavor with each new addition or subtraction. Something comes out, something goes in; nothing wasted, color and emphasis changing, rich with the blend of all things, never overwhelmed by too much of any one ingredient added.

Psychiatrists and other strip-miners of the human psyche say that you can judge a person's self-esteem, his belief in his own worth, by the way he or she dresses. If a person takes pride in having a genuinely pleasing outward appearance, it is said that the person has a justifiably good opinion of himself.

And so it seems with a city. The city, if you live in it, should be like the clothes you wear. Careful attention should be given to good taste. It should not be unkempt, dirty, neglected and unraveling. A city should be a place of trees and fountains and good lights and clean streets; of open spaces and a decent respect for its amenities. Who is going to pay for all this? You are.

In Act 2, Scene 2 of *Inherit The Wind*, the fictional Clarence Darrow stands before a jury in a dramatized version of the Scopes "Monkey Trial," and he is pleading with the jury to understand that the teaching of Darwin is no sin in the classroom. "Gentlemen, progress has never been a bargain. You've got to pay for it. Sometimes I think there is a man behind a counter who says, "All right, you can have a telephone; but you'll have to give up privacy, the charm of distance. Madam, you may vote; but at a price; you lose the right to retreat behind a powder-puff or a petticoat. Mister, you may conquer the air; but the birds will lose their wonder, and the clouds will smell of gasoline."

A city is a place where streets, parks, buildings, vistas and boulevards make up the controllable environment in which we live. We can make of it what we wish. We must be ever wary, alert to trade off carefully, aware of the costs to be paid for certain forms of progress we are offered. Every monstrous scheme or structure exacts its price, the penalty of visual blight and loss of human scale. What we have must be fiercely protected, firmly enhanced, constantly improved. Seattle has been called—perhaps with some accuracy—"the nation's most livable city." Any prediction about Seattle—what are chances?—will depend on how willing we are to shoulder the burden, not only in money, but in time, concern and often painful involvement. These are the costs you and I should be willing to assume.

We must be ready to sustain something of what Jim Ellis talked about so long ago. Ellis, an attorney who worked for many years to make our region and our city a better place in which to live, put it boldly back in 1966. It was a challenge then and it is a challenge today. It will serve for a last word here:

"We have the means and talent to create a city we want within our time. Young men and women looking for a cause beyond self can find it here. The cause is the rallying of factions, sections, races and classes to build a whole city . . . a city which will serve the needs of man and lie well in the arms of the land."

14

Mr. Thompson's Bird

Holidays are the dog days for anyone charged with writing daily. During holidays, people are busy making plans to get out of town or, if it's Christmas, they are running up big numbers on their Visa cards. Good columnists, or at least smart ones, make plans ahead and write holiday columns in advance so they are not stuck with the task of composing in the thick of everybody's holiday spirit. This never worked for me. On Labor Day it was obligatory to say something nice about the people who labor; no easy trick when you consider that old labor battles are long past, and the guy to whom you might be paying tribute is now heading off on his three-day weekend, driving his motor home, towing a boat, with two motor bikes strapped on the side. He also might be a woman.

The Fourth of July is another. The obligation here is to mix a stew of patriotism, nostalgia, warnings about firecrackers with perhaps obeisance to Mom and her famous apple pie thrown in. I always struggled with this one. For one thing, too many scoundrels in my time have used patriotism to attack the First Amendment and generally foul up the air with the kind of rhetoric which says you are disloyal if you don't believe that nerve gas is essential to the preservation of Our Way of Life. As for nostalgia, that can only take you so far, and the editorialists (also stuck for something to say) issue their own solemn warnings about the hazards of firecrackers. That leaves Mom, and it seems to me that no intelligent mother these days is going to spend her holiday baking when she can buy a perfectly good apple pie at one of a proliferation of bakeries we have spawned in the last few years.

Christmas is the worst. I am convinced that people simply give up reading newspapers the week before Christmas. I did a fair job on a couple of occasions in lathering on Christmas sentiment, but to repeat such stuff, or work variations on it for twenty years running, is more than any muse can stand. Older readers should also understand that this occupational syndrome is why newspapers used to (and still do) run that awful chestnut, "Yes, Virginia, There Is a Santa Claus."

But about twenty years ago, I stumbled on a scam that got me over Thanksgiving. Back in the late thirties there was a columnist named Morton Thompson, who wrote a funny book called *Joe, The Wounded Tennis Player*. Thompson had a swift, breezy style and he was a fellow who liked to cook. So in his book he printed his recipe for what became known, as years passed, as the Thompson Turkey. Being stuck for a column one Thanksgiving, I ran the Thompson Turkey recipe. This was long before Julia Child and James Beard and Craig Claiborne got their hooks into us; long before such spices as cumin, coriander and oregano became common-place in kitchen cupboards.

Thus, to do the Thompson Turkey, those early day readers had to chase all over town looking for poppy seed, turmeric and mace. The response in the first few years was frequently inflammatory. One guy called and threatened me with bodily harm on sight "for ruining our Thanksgiving." People called in to complain that the preparation took so long that they didn't sit down to dinner until nine. In one episode, a man and his wife, with a living room full of guests, pulled the paste-encrusted bird out and, when they tried to pull the blackened crust away, they tore all the skin off the turkey. They ended up in a screaming kitchen fight, throwing bread at each other, while the guests presumably coughed politely into their drinks in the living room.

But a curious thing began happening. About two weeks before each Thanksgiving, calls would increase, requesting a rerun of the Thompson Turkey, "because we forgot to clip and save the recipe from last year." Some of the callers were phoning long distance. Letters arrived with similar requests, some with tips on modifying the recipe. And as Thanksgiving followed Thanksgiving, the complaints lessened. I could only surmise that it was because more people, having joined the Julia Child cult of gourmet cuisine, felt at ease with Mr. Thompson's complicated creation. Certainly there were more specialty stores and gourmet shops available, so such things as turmeric and coriander were quickly available or kept on hand. So I always looked forward to Thanksgiving with joy, since it meant merely rerunning the Thompson Turkey. This took about twenty minutes to type up and it meant a day off without striving to re-create the old "to grandmother's house we go" type of column each year. I revere the memory of Morton Thompson. As for the recipe itself, it probably never will run in the dear old *P–I* again, so this is my last shot with it.

A few cautionary notes are in order. Architects of the big bird should remember that turkeys themselves have changed in the forty-plus years since the Thompson Turkey was launched. Modern birds, being more scientifically raised and fed different diets, are said to cook a bit faster than the turkeys of the thirties. A sixteen to twenty-two pound size, as stated in the recipe, is about right for this scrimmage. Oven temperatures do vary, so watch that.

Remember, this recipe comes to you only with the poetic instructions first created by Mr. Thompson. Done correctly, the Thompson Turkey is a joy. Over the years I have modified certain instructions in the recipe according to reader suggestions or complaints. Good luck to all:

Rub a sixteen to twenty-two pound bird inside and out with salt and pepper. In a stew pan put the chopped gizzard, liver, the neck and the heart, to which add one bay leaf, one teaspoon of paprika, a half teaspoon of coriander, a clove of garlic, four cups of water, and salt to taste. Let this simmer while you go ahead with the dressing.

Dice one apple and one orange in a bowl and add to this bowl a large can of crushed pineapple, the grated rind of one-half lemon, one can of drained water chestnuts, three tablespoons of chopped preserved ginger. (Editor's note—cut drastically or eliminate ginger.)

In another bowl, put two teaspoons of Colman's mustard, two teaspoons of caraway seed, three teaspoons of celery seed, two teaspoons of poppy seed, two and a half teaspoons of oregano, one well-crushed teaspoon of mace (Ed.'s note—cut down or eliminate the mace), four or five finely minced cloves of garlic, four cloves (minus heads and well-chopped), one-half teaspoon of turmeric, four large well-chopped onions, six well-chopped stalks of celery, one-half teaspoon savory and one tablespoon of poultry seasoning. Salt to taste.

In another bowl, dump three packages of bread crumbs. Add three-quarters pound of ground veal and one-quarter pound of fresh pork, a quarter pound of butter and all the fat (first rendered) you can pry loose from the turkey.

Mix the contents of each bowl. When each bowl is well mixed, mix the three of them together. And mix well. Mix it until your forearms and wrists ache. Then mix it some more. Now toss it enough so that it isn't any longer a doughy mass.

Stuff your turkey, but not too full. Skewer the bird. Turn on your oven full force and let it get red hot. Put your bird breast down on a rack.

In a cup, make a paste consisting of the yolks of two eggs, a teaspoon of Colman's mustard, a clove of minced garlic, a tablespoon of onion juice, a half teaspoon of lemon juice and enough sifted flour to make a stiff paste. Take a pastry brush or an ordinary paint brush and stand by. (Ed.'s note—increase the paste by half; you may need it.)

Put your bird in the red-hot oven. Let it brown all over. Remove the turkey. Turn your oven down to 325 degrees. Now, while the turkey is sizzling hot, paint it all over with the paste.

Put it back in the oven. The paste will set in a few minutes. Drag it out again. Paint every nook and cranny of it once more. Put it back in the oven. Keep doing this until you haven't any more paste left. (Ed.'s note—be sure and have enough paste; see above.)

To the giblet-neck-liver-heart gravy that has been simering, add one cup of cider. Don't let it cook any more. Stir it well. Keep it warm on top of the stove. This is your basting fluid.

Baste the bird every fifteen minutes. That means you will baste it from twelve to fifteen times. Turn it on its back the last half hour. It ought to cook four and one-half to five and one-half hours. When you remove it, the turkey will be dead black. You will think, "I've ruined it!"

Be calm. Take a tweezer (Ed.'s note—or small tongs) and pry loose the paste coating. It will come off readily. Beneath this burnt, harmless, now worthless shell, the bird will be golden and dark brown, succulent, giddy-making with wild aroma, crisp and crackling.

The meat beneath will be wet, juice will spurt from it in tiny fountains high as the handle of the fork plunged into it. You do not have to be a carver to eat this turkey. Speak harshly to it and it will fall apart.

And that, dear friends, is the classic Thompson Turkey. Increasingly, as the years have gone by with repeats of this recipe, tributes have poured in. A few complaints, but mostly hosannahs. Many people are now veterans of the Thompson Turkey, wouldn't cook it any other way. By now, I suspect, hundreds, if not thousands, of kitchens in Seattle have this recipe clipped and filed away. If not, this is your final reading as far as I'm concerned.

This scrumptious bird, this joy of creation, this splendid

edifice is a tribute to our never-ending pursuit of elegant dining. It sounds so good that someday I may even try it myself.